Remember Not

My Journey in Forgiveness

Hannah Lake

WESTBOW
PRESS®
A DIVISION OF THOMAS NELSON
& ZONDERVAN

Copyright © 2021 Hannah Lake.

All rights reserved. No part of this book may be used or reproduced by any means, graphic, electronic, or mechanical, including photocopying, recording, taping or by any information storage retrieval system without the written permission of the author except in the case of brief quotations embodied in critical articles and reviews.

WestBow Press books may be ordered through booksellers or by contacting:

WestBow Press
A Division of Thomas Nelson & Zondervan
1663 Liberty Drive
Bloomington, IN 47403
www.westbowpress.com
844-714-3454

Because of the dynamic nature of the Internet, any web addresses or links contained in this book may have changed since publication and may no longer be valid. The views expressed in this work are solely those of the author and do not necessarily reflect the views of the publisher, and the publisher hereby disclaims any responsibility for them.

Scripture taken from the New King James Version® Copyright © 1982 by Thomas Nelson. Used by permission. All rights reserved.

Any people depicted in stock imagery provided by Getty Images are models, and such images are being used for illustrative purposes only. Certain stock imagery © Getty Images.

ISBN: 978-1-6642-2022-5 (sc)
ISBN: 978-1-6642-2021-8 (hc)
ISBN: 978-1-6642-2023-2 (e)

Library of Congress Control Number: 2021901562

Print information available on the last page.

WestBow Press rev. date: 01/27/2021

Dedication

This book is dedicated first to the Lord, who taught me what forgiveness was, and inspired me to write the story about my journey. He has led me every step of the way, providing the strength I needed, and the faith to trust Him completely.

I dedicate this book also, to my precious momma, who was my protector, my encourager, and my great, shining example of womanhood. Her advice to me so many years ago, has rung loudly in my heart, giving me the motto that would carry me through so much in my life. She told me, "Don't judge people too quickly. There is always a reason why, behind the things that people do."

She was a steady ship on high seas, fearless and unsinkable. Life had been hard and cruel, and yet she remained a lady through it all. She went home to Jesus late, last year, just as lovely in her old age as she was all through her life.

Thank you for everything, and "Vaya con Dios" (go with God), sweet Momma, your little redhead, Hannah.

Epigraph

For I will forgive their iniquity, and their sin I will remember no more. (Jeremiah 31:34b)

Contents

Dedication v
Epigraph vii
Preface xi
Acknowledgments xiii

1. Uncovered 1
2. Finding Jesus 3
3. Sowers of Seed 8
4. Light and darkness 11
5. Hope Deferred 13
6. God Answers! 17
7. Our Courtship 19
8. A Simple Wedding 23
9. Our Honeymoon 27
10. A Blessing from God 29
11. A Turning Point 33
12. Twice Blessed 35
13. A Name from Heaven 38
14. Mothering Two 41

15. A New Direction	45
16. God Protects Our Children	51
17. Loving Our Neighbors	58
18. A Fiery Trial	60
19. Tares in the Wheat	64
20. A Troubling Dream	72
21. Our Home	74
22. A Gift	77
23. Forgiving Myself	81
24. A Mysterious Dream	85
25. My Precious Grandma	89
26. My Birth Father	96
27. I Want My Momma!	99
28. Reconciliation	103
29. Grandma Goes Home	108
30. Why, God?	112
31. A New Calling	115
32. Blessings from God	119
33. Tragedy Strikes	122
34. Dark Memories Revealed	129
35. My Sweet Momma	135
36. Forgive as We Have Been Forgiven	140
About the Author	143

Preface

I was compelled to write this book, after realizing how many others had experienced the type of trials that I had. I wanted to give them the hope, that they may be able to lay their unforgiveness down at the feet of Jesus one day too.

The Lord spoke to me through His word, in dreams and during prayer, that I must write this book so that others could be encouraged through it. It is because of my love for my savior that I obey His call, with the prayer that others indeed, may be helped.

I offer this book to every wounded soul who has been harmed by others, and I pray that each of you can find the freedom that comes when we surrender our unforgiveness to Him.

Acknowledgments

I would like to acknowledge the support and encouragement of my husband, Henry; daughter, Claire; and son, Gabriel. Without their constant support, this book would have never come to be. I am forever grateful for each of them in my life.

Uncovered

How could I ever forgive such a thing? The memories came back like deadly fumes under a door jam. They nauseated and horrified me. My heart raced, and I felt as if I were dying. I could not breathe. This would be a hard journey! There were many other times in my life that I would learn about forgiveness and be led to forgive. But this journey was long in coming, built on a foundation of mercy that the Lord gave me, which taught me how to have mercy and forgive others. A lifelong journey, as the potter shaped me with His hands into something He could use.

How can we be of use to the Lord if we have never suffered

and realized our desperate need for Him? How can we have compassion for others if we have never needed compassion ourselves? It is a truth that experience is the best teacher, and I had a lot to learn!

The Lord was allowing the memories to be uncovered so I could know the truth and, with full understanding, release those "fumes," turning them into the sweet fragrance of the forgiveness of Christ.

It took a lifetime before the Lord allowed the memories to return; for several years they came, unannounced, relentless, searing memories, as I clung fast to the robes and feet of my savior, Jesus.

Finding Jesus

I have loved my savior from the moment I received His forgiveness as an eighteen-year-old harlot. A harsh title but a truthful one.

I was raped at fourteen years old, the summer before my freshman year. I told no one. I had already told my friends lies about how "experienced" I was, so I couldn't tell them the truth. I would not tell my parents because I didn't want the man, who was not a stranger, to get in trouble. Realizing I was no longer a virgin, I allowed whatever advances from others that came my way. I just didn't care anymore.

It was the sixties, and although I tried different drugs a few times, I did not like them. They didn't fill the emptiness inside my heart, but neither did my promiscuity! My high school years passed in a dark blur of late-night trysts with strangers that led to a black, empty chasm in my soul. The emptiness grew deeper and darker after an abortion at seventeen. I started flirting with suicide, dreaming of walking into the ocean waves at night and allowing myself to be swallowed whole by the darkness consuming me. I wrote poetry, and in one poem I described myself as a beautiful, empty coffin. Lovely on the outside but empty on the inside. I was acutely aware that I was missing the most important thing in my life, but I had no idea what that was! It was the "age of Aquarius," where everyone seemed to be seeking paradise in some way, but for me, I knew it was a matter of life and death. I was so very lost!

In my senior year, I had to get a job, and found one at a doughnut shop a few blocks away from our house, where they offered me the night shift. I made fast friends with a girl a year older than me who was also working there. I did not get along so well with the cook. John was only a few years older and a nice guy, but he was also one of the "Jesus People." We worked many shifts together, and he never lost the opportunity to tell me about Jesus. He was gentle in spirit, and was not pushy, but I did *not* want to hear about Jesus!

I had a girlfriend who meant a lot to me. She told me that I had better never become a Christian or it would be over between us. She had a good friend who accepted Christ and left to become an evangelist. She felt betrayed and abandoned. Not wanting to upset her, I listened reluctantly to John as he told me how much God loved me and how Jesus died for my sins. *He has no idea how sinful I am!* I thought to myself. He told me once that I may as well accept Christ now because God had already told him that I belonged to Him! Oh, that really made me angry! I dreaded going to work! But he never gave up on me.

Then all my hopes and dreams died when my boyfriend broke up with me. He was headed to college, and his best friend told him to drop his current girlfriend so they could be free to date in college. He was apologetic, but he broke up with me just the same. I thought he was the one I would marry! He was the only thing that kept me from a watery grave. So I was resigned to walk out into the waves and sink into the cold depths forever. I had nothing left to hold on to, no reason to go on, and no hope for the future. It was all swept away with his goodbye.

Somehow I found myself at the doughnut shop when John was there with two of his friends. I must have known that, despite my doubts, he would know a way out of the deep despair that held me captive. He greeted me with his big smile and invited me to sit with them, and through tears I told him about my boyfriend. He listened calmly, and then he told me that no one could love me as much as Jesus does. He told me how the

Lord could fill up the emptiness inside my heart and save me from the darkness that held me captive. "Just say yes to Jesus." He encouraged me.

The Spirit was calling me, and tears flowed as I started to soften. Then he asked if I would like him and his friends to pray for me, and I bolted! I ran out as fast as I could and cried as I ran all the way home. I worked the night shift that night, so I had to get some sleep. But how could I sleep? My life was over! In desperation, I knelt at my bedside, took a deep breath, and prayed the prayer for salvation that John had told me about many times. I thought it was a magic prayer, a way of switching camps from Satan to Jesus. I expected thunder and lightning bolts and jumped into bed covering my head, not knowing what would happen. Nothing. Nothing happened because I was just reciting words; I had not surrendered my life to Christ. I was just seeking a quick way out of my misery. *Well, that was stupid!* I thought, and I shrugged it all off.

A few nights later, toward the end of my shift, John came in and asked me if I wanted to go with him and his friends for a ride. I thought, *Cool! That sounds like fun!* So I hopped in his car and off we went. They were all so happy and excited, and I liked being with them. Then they pulled into the parking lot of a small church for an evening worship service. I laughed to myself, thinking that was pretty sneaky. *I might as well go in,* I thought, *and make John happy.*

I was not prepared for what happened. I was shocked to see hundreds of young people packed into the small chapel. We found seats at the very back against the wall. John and his friends were the farthest thing in my mind at that moment because I sensed what seemed to be a thick, warm presence in the room. I somehow understood that the presence was in each of the people there and that it wanted inside me! I felt like a dry, empty egg shell that was about to burst from the pressure of the presence that wanted in! I did not understand what was happening or what I was experiencing, but it seemed so clear to me that I must let Him in and that He would fill the emptiness inside me. I was sobbing and broken, not knowing what to do, and then I heard the pastor ask if those who wanted to receive Christ as their savior would stand. I jumped to my feet, and as I did, I was flooded with the presence of the Holy Spirit! It felt as if I was standing under the full force of Niagara Falls! I was crying tears of joy as I relished every second of that indwelling of the Spirit. I knew I was washed. I knew I was clean. I knew my sins had been forgiven and that I was a new creation in Christ Jesus!

Then I washed you in water; yes, I thoroughly washed off your blood, and I anointed you with oil. (Ezekiel 16:9)

Sowers of Seed

Many others beside John had shared Christ with me before that night. Earlier that year on my eighteenth birthday, my boyfriend took me downtown, and we found a parking spot next to a park in the middle of town. I was mesmerized by a small gypsy wagon in the middle of the park, and a small old man with a big smile beckoned me to him. His sweet manner and kindness drew me to him. His wagon was full of Christian tracts and small Bibles. He told me that Jesus loved me, and he shared the gospel with me. I thought to myself, *Does he know what a sinner I am?* But his loving words kept me there, as he told me how Jesus died for my sins. Then he gave me a small New Testament and told me to read the book of John. He quoted Isaiah 1:18 to me, which says, "'Come now, and let us reason together,' says the LORD, 'Though your sins are like scarlet, They shall be as white as snow; Though they are red like crimson, They shall be as wool.'" Then he wrote that verse out in the front cover of the Bible he had given me. I remembered him that night, when I surrendered my life to Christ, as I realized my sins indeed, had been washed as white as snow!

A young classmate had also shared Christ with me that year, and in a sour mood, I snapped back at her, spitting out my anger, and made her cry. Her name was Ann; a sweet girl with a sparkling smile and a kind heart. She also had very thick glasses, with poor vision. She knew me from one of our high school classes. I should have felt bad about making her cry, but I didn't. Now that I had accepted Christ, God arranged a reunion!

They asked those who had accepted Christ to go to the prayer room, where they would tell us about our new life in Christ, explaining what it meant to be a child of God. They gave us a Bible, and encouraged us to read it daily, to pray, and to go to church so we could fellowship with other believers. I didn't know that many from the service, liked to greet the new believers as they came out of the prayer room. And when the door opened, there was a huge crowd, joyously greeting us and praising God. Despite the throng, all I could see was sweet Ann! She was right in front of me, but did not recognize me because of her poor vision. I cried out, "Ann!" And with a look of shock she said, "Hannah?" "Yes!" I cried, hugging her and apologizing over and over how sorry I was for making her cry. Oh, the mercy and the goodness of God! He is so wonderful! She had shared the gospel in sweet faith, and the Lord put her there that night, to see the fruit of the seeds she had planted! I am overwhelmed, just thinking about the wonderful ways that God works!

> *In the morning sow your seed, and in the evening do not withhold your hand; for you do not know which will prosper, either this or that, or whether both alike will be good. (Ecclesiastes 11:6)*

Light and darkness

As usually happens after a victory in the Lord, the enemy comes along. I got a call from my girlfriend. She had left her family home and rented an apartment on her own. She was going to have a party and wanted me to come. I did not want to upset her, even though I had told her about accepting Jesus, I wanted to prove I would not leave her. She drove me to her apartment driving in silence until we arrived, and there were maybe eight or ten people waiting. She didn't have much money, so others had brought some snacks. I had an ominous sense of dread as she was acting distant and strangely preoccupied. Then she announced that they would be having a séance.

A chill went down my spine, and I fought the urge to flee. I should have! I was only two weeks old in the Lord, and was torn between being supportive of my friend or a witness for Christ. I sat quietly praying to myself as it began, and not long into it, a cold, rushing wind blew the doors and windows open, and my friend broke out into maniacal laughter! She was babbling out of her mind, as she spun around the room laughing. Then she disappeared, running out of the apartment. I couldn't wait to get out of there! There was a friend I knew there that offered to drive me home. We talked about how crazy that was, and we both worried about what had happened to our friend. I never saw her again, and I realize that was a good thing! I found out later that she was fine, and doing her own thing. It was a good lesson in not fellowshipping with darkness! I felt guilty at first, thinking that it had all happened for my benefit. But later I realized that she had chosen darkness, and maybe one day she would choose the light.

> *Do not be unequally yoked together with unbelievers. For what fellowship has righteousness with lawlessness? And what communion has light with darkness? (II Corinthians 6:14)*

Hope Deferred

I buried myself in the Word and prayer, and never lost an opportunity to go to church. I had a friend from high school, who also had accepted Jesus as his Savior, and he gave me rides to church. One morning, while waiting at the large picture window in our living room for him to arrive, I felt so alone, wondering how my life would turn out, and I prayed: "Lord, please let me know that everything will be alright!" The words had barely left my lips when a white Dove suddenly appeared, hovering in front of me on the other side of the window. Then just as suddenly, it flew away! The Holy Spirit had given me an answer! I now knew, that God had my life in His hands, and I had no need to fear.

I was invited to a good friend's wedding, and I went alone, not having a boyfriend. I had dated a few times, non-believers, but they were disasters, and only by the grace of God I escaped unscathed! My friend's wedding was amazing! I will never forget the Southern ball gown she wore, with large hoop slip, making her look like a living doll! Her tall handsome husband, the one who had courted her from youth, gazing so lovingly at her, keeping his eyes fixed on her. I was so happy for her! But I yearned for my own true love. After the wedding was over, I slipped away in tears. I felt like an old maid. I wasn't even twenty yet! But my good friends had already married, and I was alone. I decided to increase my time in fellowship with other believers. I tried home Bible studies, and went to every service I could at church. I had a used car I bought with cash from my doughnut shop earnings and the guidance of my Daddy (my step-father), and was free to go when I wanted. My focus was on finding a husband. I thought that once you have Jesus, then you need a husband. The hunt was on! But the Lord was not cooperating with my plans. I felt strangely isolated no matter where I went! Church services, home studies, it felt as if I were in a glass bubble. I could see others, but no one seemed to be able to see me. It was as if I were a specter, there in spirit, but not in body. I could not understand why God was isolating me! The loneliness was so painful; I just buried myself in the Bible. I could not get enough of it! I was soaking up every word, deep into my longing spirit. I loved the word of God! I was growing in faith and understanding, and sought every chance to read it. During that first year after accepting Christ, a man named Henry, came into the doughnut shop just about every day. He was enamored with me and would try to make small talk, but being shy and frightened of rejection, he would stumble over his words, say the wrong thing, and I would send him out, rejecting his attempts. Eventually, he would just sit in the back, pretending to look at Hot Rod magazines, as he longed to just be there near me. I did not like him! He was too sweet, too shy, for a tall manly built man. I wanted to be swept off my feet, not gently wooed! I accepted his request for a date once, when he said we would be going on a long, scenic drive to a small, tourist town with his car club. That sounded fun! So, I went, and he was so thrilled! His buddies in the car club were amazed he had a date, because he was so shy. We had a wonderful time! Hot pretzels with crockpot cheddar cheese, souvenirs, and a wonderful dinner. On the drive home, I played up the Hay Fever attack I was having, to be worse than it was, in order to get out of kissing him good-night. He was gracious and kind, accepting my cool good-bye. I told my mom and she was angry with me. "After that wonderful date?" she exclaimed. I told her I didn't like him, and she asked me why. I told her it was because he was too nice, a "Momma's Boy". But she made me think, *Why don't I like him?* I certainly had no idea if he was a momma's boy. I had never seen him with his family. I was a hard nut to crack!

I had complained to my mom about not being able to find a husband, and she told me I would end up marrying the guy I least expected. So, I made a list of all the guys I didn't like, but I didn't even think to put Henry's name on that list! I could not imagine marrying *him*!

My desire for a husband was only tempered by my thirst for the word of God, prayer and church, which kept me hopeful that God would answer my prayers. Then, a year after accepting Christ, something so wonderful happened!

God Answers!

I was due to work the early shift that morning, and was awakened early as God revealed an amazing truth! I didn't need a husband! I was complete in Christ! *That* was why I had been isolated, dependent on Him alone! He wanted me to learn that He was the only thing I really needed. I was ecstatic! It was as if a heavy burden had been lifted from my shoulders. I was free in Christ! I was His bride! He was the focus of my life. I dressed quickly, floating on a cloud of joy, rejoicing over my new found freedom in Him. I sang songs of praise all the way to work and was full of thankfulness, ready to work! Our little doughnut shop was a very busy place in the morning.

Long lines went out into the parking lot with folks wanting their morning coffee and doughnuts. I was happily dashing from customer to coffee pot, serving Christ in joy! Then Henry walked in. It is hard to describe in words what happened, but just as I had poured a cup of coffee and held it in my hands, the Lord spoke, loudly, clearly in my ears, "Here is your husband." I almost dropped the coffee! I instinctively knew that no one else heard what God had spoken to me. I also knew it *was* God, and that what He said was a truth! It resonated in my heart, my soul, and in my spirit. In those few seconds, it was as if the world had stopped turning. The crowd became muffled, as if time itself had paused. I was looking at *my husband*! The world started turning again, the sounds of the busy shop came back and I smiled at the man before me. All my focus turned to him, and I went up to him at the counter, still smiling. He was amazed that I was smiling at him! My smile must have calmed his nerves, and he worked up the courage to ask me out, and I said, "Yes!" He was overjoyed, and so was I. God had to teach me that He was the focus of my life, and that anything He allowed in my life was for His glory, not my own! I was the Lord's servant, and He had a plan for me! Gratefully, Henry was a part of that plan! My shift flew by! Henry prepared for our date, and I started planning a wedding!

Our Courtship

Henry was tall, dark, and handsome! He was also quite shy! There was a young boy, about thirteen, who also hung out at the doughnut shop. We called him "Little Bobby", and he became our Cupid! He would take messages from Henry to me, and from me to Henry. Bobby asked me what my favorite flower was, and I had no idea! So I said, "blue Carnations." A day later, Henry drove up to the doughnut shop on his motorcycle with Little Bobby on the back, holding a big bouquet of blue Carnations!

During that time, I was concerned that Henry was not a Christian. I trusted Jesus enough to believe what He had told me, but knew I could not marry Henry until He had accepted Christ as his Savior. I witnessed to Henry every chance I got, marked a bunch of verses in the little New Testament the Gypsy man had given me, and kept it with me to share with him on dates. But Henry didn't quite understand how he could be a "sinner!" After all, he had never murdered anyone or done anything evil. It was a hard concept for him to understand. It is hard to realize you need a savior when you don't know that you are a sinner!

> *For all have sinned and fall short of the glory of God. (Romans 3:23)*

I asked him to go to church with me many times before he finally agreed, and went with me to church for an evening service. It was the right night, the right time, and the Spirit moved him! He accepted Christ as his Savior that night. Then, excited about what had just occurred, not wanting the night to end, we went to a park near the doughnut shop, and started swinging on the swings. I love swinging, and Henry pushed me high into the night sky. With the cool air rushing by me, I was thrilled! As we swung together, he stopped swinging, and became silent. I knew what was coming, and I panicked, not knowing what to do! I prayed, "Lord! I don't feel fireworks with him the way I did with other guys, what do I do?" I felt the

Spirit saying, "Say, 'Yes!'" I did feel happy and safe with him, so I kept praying for guidance. Then Henry said, "I love you." Flustered, I said, "That's nice!" "You don't understand." He said, "I have never said that to anyone, not even my mother." I kept swinging. "Will you marry me?" He said, his head bowed down. God clearly told me, "Say, 'Yes!'" But I responded with, "Sure!" Poor Henry! I'm sure he did not expect such a casual response! Surprised by my answer, he asked me, "Can I fall out of the swing now?" We held hands as we walked back to the doughnut shop; we didn't even kiss afterwards. But I had such peace! I knew this was what God wanted for us and I trusted Him. I felt warm, safe, and so very happy. It was June, and we excitedly talked about our plans for the future and what each of our expectations were, as he drove me home to meet his folks. He was surprised to find the house dark when we went in, then Henry remembered that his folks were visiting his aunt and uncle who lived out of town. So he called them, and really gave them a shock! He had never even told them he was dating anyone! When I got home, I woke my folks and told them I was engaged. Momma was calm, as if she had expected it, but her giggle told me she was pleased.

Shortly after our engagement, Henry came into the doughnut shop with a three-pack of Cracker Jacks. He had opened one and offered me one too. I was excited, because they used to have real little surprises in them! I always dug out the surprise before eating them. I opened the little paper sack, to find a golden metal wedding band! It was engraved and looked real, except for the opening so it would fit. We had not purchased our wedding rings yet, so I put on the simple ring and wore it proudly until my wedding ring set was ready. I still have that little gold band! It's as shiny and new looking as the day I opened the Cracker Jacks, so many years ago!

We planned to get married the following June, but that was *so* far away! We were so eager to be together forever. Out of our parent's homes and into our own. We moved the date up to February, and then again to October, just a few months away! We knew our folks could not afford a big wedding, so we decided to just make it a small wedding with only our immediate family members. Then, I went with my mom, my brother and sister to see my Uncle Ted and Aunt Tammy. They were running a little café in another town, and they were delighted to see us! When I told my uncle about our plan to only have immediate family members, he was shocked! We had always been quite close, and he was my favorite uncle. Such a bright, happy, positive man. "Oh no!" He said, "You can't do that." "You have family members who love you! They should all be able to come!" I realized what he was saying was true. Him and Aunt Tammy offered to help in any way they could. I think mom was relieved to have help with the planning too. So, we decided to invite our close relatives and friends, as it should be!

A Simple Wedding

I decided to sew my own dress, not just to save money, but because I wanted it to be *my* dress. Momma, always the perfect hostess, planned to host the reception in our home, utilizing the large backyard with a beautiful covered patio, that Daddy had made. My Aunt Tammy gave me the gift of the wedding cake of my choice! Her mother was a Wedding Cake Baker! I choose a three-tier cake at her urging, with blue roses. When it came to my flowers, I swooned over the different floral choices. But ended up sticking with the less expensive carnations and daisies. It turned out to be a perfect match for my dress!

It was a country-style wedding dress, with an Empire waist, long puffy sleeves, a large flounce around the hem, and all in white, dotted Swiss. I used a blue centered daisy trim, keeping with the blue theme. Blue was Henry's favorite color too. It was just perfect! Henry had asked his brother, Steven to be his Best Man, and I had asked my friend, Laura to be my Maid of Honor. My brother and sister were the Ring Bearer and Flower Girl. My uncles and Henry's father all stepped up on the day of the ceremony serving as ushers. Henry looked amazing in his properly fitted suit! Before I knew it, I was walking down the aisle on the arm of my Daddy! The altar was several steps up, and when we had our rehearsal the church coordinator told me I had better take a huge handful of dress up in my hands or I would not clear the steps! She told of brides who had stepped on the hems of their dresses, and the dresses had torn lose from the bodice! Once Daddy had given my hand to Henry, I took what I thought it was a big enough handful of my dress as I stepped up onto that first step, but it was not enough! I had stepped firmly on the hem of my dress! Our Pastor must have seen the panic in my eyes, but before I could stumble, Henry's sure arm held me steady! My full weight was on his arm as I took each step on the hem of that dress, unable to clear it! The bodice strained at the pressure as I took each step. Finally, I was on level ground. And no one watching, except those in front of us, knew that there was any problem! My husband carried me so smoothly on his arm, no one knew. I was so thankful for his calm, steady presence. And for the strength of the dress I had made! I don't think a store-bought dress could have stood up to that test. Our pastor's smile beamed throughout the service, and we were married.

So then, they are no longer two but one flesh. Therefore what God has joined together, let not man separate. (Matthew 19:6)

As we walked back down the aisle as man and wife, my little brother, overcome with emotion, buried his face in the ring pillow to hide his tears. I treasure that tear stained pillow. He is with Jesus now.

Momma had set up a lovely buffet in their backyard. All of our family and friends were there. The cake was perfect, and we all had a wonderful time together. I'm so thankful for my Uncle Ted's insistence on having the whole family there. Henry and I were hesitant to leave. I think we both were a bit frightened to think of going to our new apartment alone. But the next thing we knew, we were driving off in a hail of rice!

I will never forget how Henry carried me all the way up the stairs to our second-floor apartment! I still swoon just thinking about it! We kissed once we were over the threshold. Then we both played a game of evasion! Neither of us wanted to go into the bedroom, so we were immediately bored. Then Henry asked if we should just go back and open up our wedding gifts, and I thought that was a great idea, so I called my momma. It sounded like almost everyone was still there, and Momma nearly died laughing when I said we were bored! When she recovered, she said to come on over, and everyone in the background cheered when they knew we were coming. So, we arrived, still in our wedding clothes, and opened all our gifts with such excitement and joy! We said good-bye again, and left, but still took our time. We went to the doughnut shop to say hi, and then to Henry's store to surprise his co-workers, before we finally went home to our little nest. By that time, we were both ready to cross the threshold of our bedroom. He became my one true love that night.

> *My beloved is mine, and I am his. (Song of Solomon 2:16a)*

Our Honeymoon

Rise up, my love, my fair one,
And come away! (Song of Solomon 2:13b)

We could not afford a traditional honeymoon, so we decided to spend our honeymoon taking road trips not too far away. The first morning we headed out, stopping first for breakfast at a restaurant. We held hands across the table, gazing into each other's eyes as we waited for our food. My eyes welled up with tears as I realized the blessing God had given me in Henry. I did not deserve a wonderful husband like him. And yet in the Lord's mercy, He gave me the desire of my heart! In Bible times, I would have been stoned to death. Instead, Jesus washed all my sins away, and made me as white as snow. Allowing me to wear that sweet, white gown, as a virgin bride in the eyes of the Lord. I realized the magnificent gift of His forgiveness and of the grace that He bestowed on me and felt so humbled and grateful to be holding the hands of the wonderful man God had chosen for me. Henry was surprised at my tears, and asked if I was okay, and all I could say was how I loved him, and how happy I was to be his wife. I still am!

A Blessing from God

After two years, I really wanted a baby, but was having trouble conceiving. For my twenty-first birthday at winter time, Henry reserved a little cabin in the mountains, knowing how much I loved the snow! It was a small, cozy cabin, with a fireplace, a big feather bed, and a window overlooking the falling snow. Love prevailed that night!

The next evening on my actual birthday back in town, we were at our favorite Mexican restaurant, celebrating with my family. Being now twenty-one, they brought me a Margarita. I took a sip, and was hit with a wave of nausea! Mom saw I did not look good, and asked if I was okay, so I told her about feeling nauseated. "Oh, you're pregnant!" She exclaimed delightfully. Then she told me that the only time she ever had "Morning Sickness" was twenty-four hours after conception! And she was right. A few months later I saw my doctor and I got the call a few days later, telling me I was indeed pregnant! (It took much longer then to confirm a pregnancy!) I was ecstatic! I cried, thanking God for this blessing. But that didn't last long.

My joy was swallowed up in fear, because I felt I was unworthy to have a baby. After all, I had aborted my first child. I became depressed, morose, convinced I would miscarry, or that my baby would die. The enemy knows how to take our joy, by causing us to look back on who we *were*, and keeping us from realizing who we *are* in Christ. My depression was affecting our marriage, as I had always been cheerful and positive. Henry no longer looked forward to coming home to me, and he did not feel that he loved me anymore. I was devastated! I was afraid he would leave me, like a neighbor who also was eight months pregnant, and her husband had left her! I broke down in tears, crying out to God for help. "Help me Jesus! What do I do? He doesn't love me anymore!" The Lord spoke to my heart, saying, "I put you together for a reason, don't give up." God's answer to me, put an end to my sobbing. I dried my tears, and determined to do my best to be cheerful and welcoming, when he would come home from work.

I did not miscarry, and gave birth to a beautiful baby girl, Claire, who had hair just like her daddy! I was so thankful that she was in perfect health, and so very eager to hold her and nurse her. I had told the staff that I wanted to breast-feed my baby, but the doctor frowned on that. They told me I had to wait forty-eight hours, because my "milk had to come in." They kept her in the nursery, only a short distance from my room, and for two days I listened to her crying for me. They fed her sugar water, as my breasts swelled up, aching for my baby. Finally, they pushed her bassinet in to me, and even wrapped tightly in a blanket, she had raised her chest and head up, eyes wide open, looking around, straining to find me! The nurse handed her to me and left. Finally, she was in my arms! She nursed like the starving baby she was. Despite the cruelty of the doctor's orders, she was mine! I would never allow her to be separated from me again! I would be taking her home that day. The nurse came in to give me a copy of her Birth Certificate. I was overwhelmed as I read it. Realizing the reality of it, and the mercy and love of the Lord, in giving me, an unworthy sinner, this precious baby! The baby I thought I would never have. The baby I was convinced I was not worthy of. And there, in the bathroom where I had retreated, I wept tears of joy and gave thanks to God in prayer for His forgiveness to me, and this wonderful gift!

For this child I prayed, and the Lord has granted me my petition which I asked of Him. 1 Samuel 1:27

I will never forget the ride home! Henry, in his love and protection of his precious newborn, drove twenty miles per hour all the way home!

It was about nine months later when Henry, waiting until we were going to bed at night, told me he had something to tell me. I held my breath until he said, "I love you." I said I loved him too, but he said, "No, you don't understand. I felt as if I didn't love you anymore, but now I realize how much I really do love you."

Oh, thank You Jesus! For encouraging me to stay and trusting You with our marriage! Your mercy is so amazing!

A Turning Point

We loved our little girl, but Henry rarely saw her, working over one hundred hours a week as a grocery manager. When he wasn't at work, he was getting calls at all hours of the day and night. He had no rest or peace and missed our daughter so! We were living in an apartment close to his work, so I would take our daughter in her stroller across the highway to see her daddy at work. She was a charmer and said "Hi" to everyone who approached her and she loved to shop! I would wander in the store for hours so Henry could get brief chances to see her.

Then one day Henry came home from work beaming, a big smile on his face, as he said with excitement, "I've got good news and bad news, what do you want first?" Before I could answer, fearful of what was to come, he said, "I'll give you the bad news first; I quit my job! I wrote a letter of resignation, and as I was finishing, I noticed a Christian tract on the floor, and the good news is, I rededicated my life to the Lord!" Wow! I was trying to be happy for him, but thoughts of finances were prevailing. He calmed my fears by telling me that he had a good amount accrued with the company stocks and his severance would hold us for a couple of months. He showed me a copy of his resignation, so sweet! He told them he wanted to see his daughter before she was married! And she was only two!

We packed up and moved closer to our families, into a quiet, tree-lined neighborhood. We were thankful for the one-story, two-bedroom apartment we found. Henry had been trying to find a job, but his resignation had closed the doors on any similar job. Days and weeks passed, and he still did not have any responses in his job hunt. We got down to only a small amount of money, and I felt I had to say something. I told him what was left in the bank, and asked what we were going to do. I will never forget his response, "I am trusting God, you need to too." Wow! That really blessed me. It was only a few days later that he took a job as a receiver at a different grocery store. A humble step down from management! But it was where the Lord was leading him!

Twice Blessed

One day, out of the blue, Henry said, "I would like to have another child." I was thrilled! What we didn't know, was that I was already pregnant! God answered him in a hurry! I did not worry or fret about the health of this baby. I trusted God, and did not listen to the lies of the enemy. I loved being pregnant! I was healthy and craving protein! Because of the baby's size, my doctor thought I was further along than I was, or I had twins. It turned out to be a big boy! And surprise, red hair! Just like me. I was so happy! When I was a teenager, I always said I never wanted a redhead, and especially not a redheaded boy. Due to my red hair, I had been teased mercilessly as a child, and I rarely saw a good-looking redheaded boy. There to prove me wrong, was the most beautiful, redheaded baby boy you ever saw! God is so awesome!

The room I had in the hospital, allowed the baby to be with the mom. The bassinet could slide out like a drawer for mom, and then she could push it back in for a nurse to tend to when she was tired. But they had staffing issues, so we did not have that option. Instead, they kept the babies in the nursery several floors below us. I was so disappointed, but they were good about bringing him to me for feedings every four hours. Then, only two hours after the last feeding, I woke-up suddenly in bed, knowing my baby needed me. I was getting ready to call the nurse, when I heard my boy crying, from a long distance away, and his cries were getting louder as he got closer. I thought it must be feeding time, but when I saw what time it was, I wondered what was happening. I sat up and prepared to breastfeed him, and was ready as the nurse came in with him. She was shocked to find me awake! She said they knew it was way too early for his feeding, but he seemed to want his mom really bad, so they decided to bring him to me. Then she asked, "How did you know?" I told her I woke up knowing he needed me and heard him as they approached. "But how did you know it was your baby?" She asked in awe. I replied that I instinctively knew it was him, and recognized his cry. She left amazed and confused, as he nuzzled against his momma, peaceful and content.

I was so thankful, to have easy access to my baby. I kept thinking about how hard it was, to be aching for my daughter, after she was born, as she cried for me, just a short distance away. I was missing her right then, and longing to get home!

A Name from Heaven

The next morning, we had to figure out what to name him! We had always planned to name a son after Henry's father, but it just didn't seem right to us, as we thought he needed his own name. We each said names in turn, and to each, we said, "No." We were running out of ideas when all of the sudden, at the same time, we both said, "Gabriel!" We were both so pleased with that name! And we both felt that God had whispered that name to us! Later that day, my grandma called, and asked what we named our boy. I told her "Gabriel," and she said, "Oh! You named him after grandpa!" I was stunned and amazed! Then my visit to see him, shortly before he went home to Jesus, came freshly back to me.

It was three years before, I was about eight months pregnant with our first-born, Claire, when I drove to my great-grandpa's little house, in an old section of town, to visit him. He had been a hard father in his younger years, until Jesus! Grandma told me how one day she saw her mother laying out baptism clothes on their bed, and she asked her why. Her mother told her, "Your father will accept Christ at church today." And she was right! Grandma said, as the pastor gave the altar call, her tall father stood up and walked down that aisle. She said she watched as he was baptized in the river, near their little town in the South. Grandpa became a new man that day! When I got to know him years later, he was the sweetest man. He had become blind due to diabetes, but was so cheerful! We loved having him over for family celebrations. He would play his harmonica and tap his feet as he played. He always said, "Sure smells good! I hope it tastes good too!" God had blessed him with three Christian wives, and he outlived each of them. He lived alone in his little house, and had a housekeeper who would clean, cook his meals and check in on him. As I visited with him, he asked me to please read the Scriptures to him. He said his housekeeper was not a believer, and did not know how to read the Bible. I was eager to read to him, and opened up Psalms from the Bible on his coffee table. He wept as I read, a smile on his face as he relished the word of God. He asked me later what we had planned to name our child if it was a boy, and I told him we planned to name him after Henry's father. "Oh", he sighed wistfully, "I always wanted a child named after me." He went home to Jesus, shortly after my visit, peacefully in his sleep, with a slight smile on his face. He was buried in his Salvation Army uniform, in which he was so proud to serve. I gave birth to our daughter, and forgot all about his words, until grandma reminded me. I rejoiced in the hand of God, as we both knew it was the Lord's angels that whispered that name to us, so that Grandpa Gabriel, in the presence of his Lord, would indeed have a child named after him!

Mothering Two

I was missing our daughter, Claire, so very much! She was three, and was eagerly awaiting the arrival of her new baby brother! Henry's folks brought her to the hospital, and as we came out of the elevator, me in a wheelchair with Gabriel in my arms, Claire saw us, and ran to us yelling "Mommy, Mommy!" Gabriel knew that voice! He whipped his head around trying to find where she was, as she ran up to us. It was a bond that would never be severed. Our little family was complete!

Before Gabriel came along, I always wondered how I could possibly love another child the way I loved my Claire! I found out quickly, that not only could I love him, but even favor him! I found myself being cross with Claire for the smallest things, despite her loving and doting on her brother! She never blamed him for my slights towards her, thank goodness! Henry was the very image of Christ, as he lovingly corrected me, and gave special favors to Claire. She was such a good girl! Always helping me care for Gabriel, and trying to protect him from me. He was trying to put his fingers into an electric socket and I slapped his hand telling him firmly, "No!" She ran to his defense, "Don't hit my brother!" So sweet! I explained to her the danger he was in and that I *would* punish him, to keep him from doing that again, but she was still upset with me, and cuddled her brother, distracting him away from the outlet. (We bought safety covers right away!) But we would have had to keep him in a cage to keep him out of trouble! He had no sense of fear, a curious nature, and a high pain tolerance. A perfect recipe for disaster! When he was nine months old, he loved following his sister around in his walker. They were in the enclosed front porch playing when Claire screamed for help. Gabriel had pushed his walker over the edge of a sunken planter in front of the floor to ceiling window, which threw him face first onto the window ledge, splitting his top lip! Henry worked nights, so he was sleeping, but quickly came to our aid, and drove us to the emergency room. The first of many trips! They came to know him by name! He was unfazed, and kept smiling all the way there, despite his wound! I was broken hearted! He had the sweetest, rosebud lips! And now there would be a permanent scar. Thankfully not as bad as it could have been. The doctor said if he used Novocain, it would leave a more pronounced scar, so he asked me to hold his head while he stitched. I was amazed at how unaffected Gabriel was! He hardly cried at all!

Not long after that, he learned how to climb over the railing of his crib in the highest position, and drop down to freedom! One morning I got up to find little footprints on top of the dining room table! I asked Claire what happened, and she said, "Don't worry Mommy, Gabriel got on top of the dining room table, but I got him off." What? That boy! Claire had been the very picture of femininity, being as cautious as possible to keep herself from harm, and she never saw an injury, until Gabriel came along! He really kept me on my toes, and I learned quickly to be up before him! Despite his drive for excitement, I absolutely loved being a mommy! I treasured every little second!

I was most charmed by the deep love and closeness they shared as brother and sister. They never fought, and played together for hours on end. I loved watching them interact, as Claire would help her brother, and he would follow her around, always wanting to be near her. When she started Kindergarten, he was broken-hearted! He would stand at the screen door every day of school, anxiously awaiting her return. It was such a blessing, to see the deep and lasting love they had for one another. Our children were such wonderful gifts from the Lord!

> *Behold, children are a heritage from the LORD, The fruit of the womb is a reward. (Psalm 127:3)*

A New Direction

I felt so blessed that God had provided a job for Henry, that paid enough for me to be a full-time mom. That humble job he took as a receiver at a grocery store, led to his dream vocation!

As he became familiar with the truckers delivering to the store, they told him he would only need a Class One license to apply for a job as a truck driver with the company. He had always wanted to be a truck driver! I remember how excited he was when he came home and told me. I encouraged him to ask for a loan from his folks for Truck Driving School, and they agreed! In no time, Henry had completed the course and went to apply for a job as a grocery truck driver. I was at home, praying for him, when he came through the door with a look of amazement on his face. I asked what happened, and he said, "They hired me! They actually hired me!" He went on to explain that the truck he was tested in was completely different than the one he was trained in, and he was grinding gears like crazy! When they were finished with the road test and went back to the yard, his supervisor told him to come into the office to fill out paperwork. Henry wondered why, thinking there was no way they would hire him. So, he asked why, and the supervisor said, "Because you're hired." Henry's eyes were wide with excitement. The supervisor said he was impressed with Henry's safe driving. And that he would learn the rest quickly. With his new paychecks, we were able to pay his folks back in a few months. Henry loved his job, and went on to earn many safety awards, as well as many trophies at the company sponsored Truck Rodeos, that showcased the driver's skills. One day, he was talking to an old-time trucker with the company, about when Henry was young, living overseas as a military kid, and how he loved watching and hearing the trucks wind their way up a certain, steep grade, and wished he could be a truck driver one day. The older trucker asked him about where and when it was, and when Henry told him, he said that he was driving military transport trucks, on that same stretch, at that same time! I love the way God confirms the gifts He gives us! Henry retired proudly twenty-seven years later.

Shortly after Henry was hired, the company was asking if any drivers wanted to transfer to the newly built, giant warehouse in another county. Few wanted to uproot their families, but for us it was an opportunity to move somewhere permanent. So, Henry requested the transfer, and despite his lack of seniority, he was accepted!

We found a lovely three-bedroom, two-bath home near the warehouse, in a nice quiet neighborhood. We were smitten with it, as soon as we saw it! Such a low rent too. Then we got out of the car, and saw the next-door neighbors had a little girl the same age as Claire! The house had a soaring ceiling in the living room, and a huge country kitchen. We had found our home.

We were settling in to our home, enjoying a real house, without hearing neighbors above or below us, and having windows all around, that let the light in. The kids loved having a real yard, with grass to play on, instead of the concrete slab they were used to. One day, when they were outside playing, I turned on the television, bored while Henry slept, as he was working nights as a truck driver. I couldn't find anything worthwhile, until I turned on a Gospel pastor, preaching the word of God. It captured me, because I have always loved Gospel churches. I remember clearly how excited I was to go to church when I was little, and it was a Gospel church.

There I was, sitting on the floor in front of the television, as the preacher reached down into my heart, and I wept. I missed church! We had not been going to church, due to Henry's work schedule and our move, so far away from our church. But there was a small church, at the end of our street. I determined that we should go! When it was time for Henry to wake up, I greeted him, and then said, "I'm taking the kids to church with me tomorrow, if that is okay with you?" And he replied, "Can I go too?" That began our fellowship at that small church. The pastor was friendly, and appeared to be following the word of God. We quickly made many close friends there and we both became involved in the children's ministries. Henry was also involved in the Food Bank there, taking food to those in need. Interestingly, Henry took some food to feed the homeless in the same downtown, and at the same park where the evangelist with the gypsy wagon had been, who had shared Christ with me.

He has always loved helping others. I called him my "Angel of the Highway," because when we were in the car, or even when he was driving his truck at work, he never passed a stranded motorist. He always stopped to make sure they were okay, and often made repairs or changed tires. He has always been eager to help others. I'm so thankful that his example has been a legacy for our children. They learned kindness and helpfulness from their dad.

Our children were four and seven years old, the year they

accepted Christ as their Savior. It was April in the early 1980's, when a false messiah, published a full-page ad in every major newspaper around the world! In it, he called himself the Christ, and said that he was waiting in an "inner room", and soon would make himself known to the world. Just as Jesus warned in Matthew 24:26, "Therefore, if they say to you, 'Look, He is in the desert!' do not go out; or 'Look, He is in the inner rooms!' do not believe it. For as the lightning comes from the east and flashes to the west, so also will the coming of the Son of Man be." I was so excited! I thought that if an anti-Christ was announcing his arrival, that surely it was time for Jesus to take us home! In my excitement, I went in to where our children were playing, and explained to them how to accept Jesus Christ as Lord, and then I had them pray with me to accept Christ into their hearts. I did not recognize it at first, but after a few days we saw an amazing change in our little son! We realized then, that he had been sincere with his prayer, and was saved! A short time later, my husband and I were planning to be baptized at church, because we never had been. My daughter came to me in the kitchen, and asked if she could be baptized too. I explained that it was something the Lord said we should do, to show that we belonged to Him, after we accept Him into our hearts. Then she looked up to me with questioning eyes, and said, "But won't it wash my sins away?" I was able to explain that only Jesus could wash our sins away. And our little girl, confessed that she was a sinner, and gave her life to Jesus, there, in the kitchen with me. Oh, what a blessing! She ran right outside, to tell all her friends in the neighborhood about Jesus! I was so proud of her, but a little bit embarrassed, I'm ashamed to say. She even told strangers about Jesus in the grocery store! So sweet!

> *I have no greater joy than to hear that my children walk in truth. (III John 1:4)*

Our lives became focused on our involvement with church, and life was busy and happy. We were also going to a home Bible study, hosted by one of the elders from that small, local church. We had never felt so close to the body of Christ as we did then.

God Protects Our Children

Both of our children loved playing outside, and they had their share of bumps and bruises, especially Gabriel! He had no fears, and loved riding his bike. One afternoon, I heard screaming outside, and knowing Gabriel was on his bike, I raced outside, and saw a neighbor a few doors down, across the street, crying out, "Oh Dios Mio! Oh Dios Mio!" Gabriel was standing in the street straddling his bike, a look of worry on his face, as if he was in big trouble! There was also a car stopped sideways, next to Gabriel. The woman inside seemed dazed and shocked.

I asked my Hispanic neighbor what happened, and he told me that my boy rode his bike out between two parked cars in front of his house, right into the path of a car! "There was no way the car could have missed him!" He insisted. And then he said, "All of the sudden, it was like the hand of God, came down and pushed the car sideways, away from the boy!" Then he continued to look to heaven, his hands raised, repeating, "Oh Dios Mio!" I asked the woman what happened, and she said, "I have no idea! I thought for sure I was going to hit the boy! He was right in front of me! And the next thing I knew, my car was pushed sideways, by something?" I thanked her and apologized for my son, and she said she was so very grateful that she did not hit him, and added, "I still don't understand how I didn't hit him!"

I knew! My neighbor knew! God was watching over our son!

For He shall give His angels charge over you, To keep you in all your ways. (Psalm 91:11)

This was only one of many rescues. I came to realize, that God had plans for our children.

Not too long after that, it was our daughter, that was "rescued".

It was a busy day! We were in a hurry to get groceries to make a dinner for guests arriving to our home soon. I was in my typical tunnel vision, focused on all that had to be done.

I was a poor example of Martha, in the Bible, when she was overwhelmed! We were heading to the car, and I was in a sour mood, complaining to Henry as the kids got into the truck. The large American pick-up, had a small second seat, behind the front seat, just big enough for the kids. Gabriel was safe in his seat, and I was telling Claire to hurry up! "I haven't got time for this!" I said, as I slammed the door shut. There was a whimper, as I realized it did not shut, but I had slammed our daughter's little hand in the door jamb! She couldn't breathe for the pain, and almost passed out, then she started crying out in agony! Her little hand was mangled! Her fingers were going every which way, and swelling up immediately! I ran to the fast-food place that was in the parking lot, and brought back a cup of ice water, and held her close to me in the front seat, putting her hand in the water. "Great!" I said, "Just what I need! It will take an hour to get to Emergency in this traffic!" Henry told me to calm down, but all I could do was think about how this ruined our plans for the day! I steamed as I looked away from my poor daughter, looking at my reflection in the window, disgusted with myself, realizing how awful I was acting! The ice water helped her pain, and soon she said, with a tender voice, "Momma, if I pray, can God heal me?" "Of course, He can!" I snapped back, really feeling miserable about myself, now. At that point I started to pray for God to change my heart, but it was only a minute, before Claire said, "Momma! It worked!"

"What do you mean, 'It worked?!'" I snapped back. "It doesn't hurt anymore!" She said. "Let me see your hand!" I demanded. It looked as if nothing had ever happened! I know broken fingers when I see them, and she had broken four of them for sure! Her fingers had looked like the petals of a crumpled flower! And there, was her perfect, little hand, as good as new. "Bend your fingers!" I demanded, still unbelieving what I was seeing. And her fingers were fine! Henry, Gabriel and Claire were praising God, and I was wallowing in remorse over my wickedness.

Oh, the mercy and the love of our Savior for His little ones! Oh, the faith of a little child! How wrapped up in the world and all its demands we can allow ourselves to be! As if my plans really mattered at all?

It still hurts to recall my evil response; but how wonderful to know, that despite our undeserving ways, God still forgives us! Even in the midst of my sin, He had mercy on my little daughter and healed her.

This story went forward in time, many years later, when Claire's young daughter, not much older than she had been at the time, accidently slammed the car door on her own hand! She could not open the door to get it out, due to the safety locks on the rear car doors, so Claire had to jump out and open it. She was terrified when she saw her daughter's hand! It appeared to be severely injured, so she called me, and described it to me and I told her to meet me at the hospital. She wrapped it in a damp wash cloth, and drove her to the emergency department. While she drove, she told her daughter what had happened to her when she was little, and how Jesus healed her when she prayed. Then they prayed together as they approached the hospital. When they took the cloth off of her hand in the emergency room, her hand appeared fine! There was no evidence of the severe injury that had been quite visible! God had healed her too! God hears the cries of His children!

But Jesus said, 'Let the little children come to Me, and do not forbid them; for of such is the kingdom of heaven.' (Matthew 19:14)

As Gabriel grew older, he became more adventurous, testing the boundaries of safety on a daily basis! His bike, now a BMX bike, was the source of many injuries, but taken in stride, and with great enthusiasm! Stitches were nothing to him, and I learned to take them out myself, to spare us another trip to the doctor. When he was a teenager, he took a hard fall on his knee at the BMX track, and it swelled up fast. He said it hurt bad, and being unlike him to complain of pain, I knew he had to be seen. I took him to the emergency room, and they were really packed! But they got an x-ray as soon as we got there. It was a long wait for the doctor, and he was in a lot of pain. So I put my hand above his knee, which was covered by a sheet, and prayed for God to heal him, and to take away the pain. Almost immediately, he fell into a deep sleep. I was grateful, and continued to pray while we waited. After what seemed like hours, the doctor came in after viewing the x-ray at the entrance to the room. "Now let me see that knee." He said, as he lifted the sheet. I was amazed and so was he, as he questioned, "Is this the right knee?" There was no swelling at all! Gabriel verified, that it was the right knee, and the doctor checked both knees to be certain, and then he quickly went out to look at the x-ray again. But, instead of coming back in, I heard him demand a new x-ray to be taken, saying, "This can't be right!" Then we were left to wait again. I asked Gabriel how he felt, and he said he felt fine, and had no pain! After the second x-ray, the doctor discharged Gabriel, without commenting. He sent the nurse in to tell us we could go, because there was no evidence of an injury! When we got to the car, Gabriel told me that God was calling him into the ministry. "How do you know?" I asked. Then he told me how his youth pastor had shared with the youth group, that he knew God was calling him, but he didn't want to quit running track, which had become quite important to him. After ignoring God's call for a while, his knee went out on the track, and he had to stop. That is when he finally answered the call of God. Gabriel said, that in the emergency room, God brought that story back to mind, and he understood why. But Gabriel also expressed concern, that he too, wanted to have fun now, and that he wasn't ready to serve God yet. I was excited, and was praying for him, and went to one of my favorite pastors at our old home church. He had counseled Henry and I before our marriage, and was not afraid to speak the truth. He listened as I told him the story, and then, after a pause, he told me, "He will fall away, like many of our pastors here, who heard the call of God in their youth, and were drawn away by the world for a time. But you, mother, pray! That is what God is calling you to do, and he will come back in God's timing." That was not what I expected to hear! I was shaken by his words. This pastor had walked for many years with the Lord, and was as grounded in the word, as any man could be. So, I received what he said, and I prayed! And what he said, indeed happened.

It would be 14 years, of earnest prayers for our son, before he embraced God's call in his life. God saved his life many times during those years, and several times afterwards! God choses us, and sees our path, when we do not know what may lay before us. He is always with us, and He is faithful!

> *Fear not, for I am with you;*
> *Be not dismayed, for I am your God.*
> *I will strengthen you,*
> *Yes, I will help you,*
> *I will uphold you with my righteous right hand. (Isaiah 41:10)*

Loving Our Neighbors

Henry and I got along well with our neighbors. They were quite friendly and good, honest people. We enjoyed birthday parties and other celebrations together. Then one day, our pastor from the small local church, asked us if we had been sharing the gospel with our neighbors. We were surprised, and said no, but that we were friendly, and treated them as brothers and sisters. The pastor then told us, that one of our neighbors came to him, and said that he had been a Christian, but had fallen away, and he wanted to return to Jesus, and have the joy that he saw in us. He rededicated his life to the Lord, and we saw a wonderful change in him, reconciling with his wife and children. It was not long after that, when our neighbor was killed in a tragic accident. We were shocked, and heartbroken for his family, but we were also so thankful for the forgiveness of Christ! Just to think, that Christ would not leave His lost sheep in the wilderness, but as a good Shepherd He would go after him! He brought His prodigal son back, so that he would return to faith in Christ, before he was called home.

> *For you were like sheep going astray, but have now returned to the Shepherd and Overseer of you souls. (I Peter 2:25)*

Our connection to all our neighbors grew closer, as we sought to comfort his family, and each other with every trial that came to each of us.

We know that we are to share the love of Christ with all we know, but something like this helped us see the urgency of letting others know about the forgiveness they can have through Jesus Christ. It helped us in our daily walks, to be mindful of how short a time we may have, and not to waste a moment of it.

A Fiery Trial

I had been having abdominal pain that was increasing, and it was determined by the gynecologist that I needed a hysterectomy. I was eager to end the pain, and had no hesitation as surgery approached. As I was wheeled towards surgery, I started singing, "Have I not commanded you? Be strong and of good courage; do not be afraid, nor be dismayed, for the LORD your God is with you wherever you go." Joshua 1:9, put to song by the local pastor's wife for our women's Bible study. Then, as they prepared to put me to sleep, I asked if I could pray first, and they all agreed. I prayed for the doctors and the nurses and for guidance and blessing, and when I finished and opened my eyes, the whole room had their heads bowed in prayer! That was the last thing I saw, before I was shocked awake by such searing pain, pain beyond anything I had ever experienced in my life! It felt as if I were on fire! My first instinct was to jump off the table and flee from the pain, and it took several nurses to hold me down and strap me in place. I was wide awake, my eyes wide open in panic, the pain was scorching my body beyond comprehension. They were injecting pain medicines, but nothing seemed to touch it. With me still quite sedated from anesthesia, I was not thinking clearly. All I could comprehend was the pain, and I thought that if I could get out of the room, the pain would stop. I was alert to everything that was being said, to try to find a way out. Then I heard them ask someone else who was recovering, what day it was, and he said, "Friday". Frantically I tried to memorize it, "Friday!" Then they asked what his name was, and I had to think, "What's my name?" I finally remembered, "It's Hannah!" I thought. Then I was pleading with God, "Please! Let them ask me! Let them ask me!" Soon they did! "Friday!" I almost answered before they asked me! "Hannah!" So eager to leave the room of pain! And then they called for someone to transport me to my room. I will never forget the horror I felt, as the elevator doors closed, and the pain was still there! I was wild with pain and frantic to escape, hoping it would all go away soon. When they got me to my room, and the nurses came in, I could not respond to them; all I could say was *"Hurt!"* They checked my vital signs and I heard them say, "She never should have been brought down here this way!" They gave me a pain medicine injection in my hip, and it started to take the edge off of the pain, but still not enough to end my agony! I was pressing my head so hard into the side rails, that I ended up with bruises from it. The kind nurse who prepared me for surgery the night before, told me, if I was hurting, I had to speak up and tell them. So when I would become conscious again, I would call out *"Hurt!"* While this went on, I managed to get my eyes open briefly, and saw a beautiful bouquet on my side table, with three small balloons, that had the words, "Praise the Lord" on them. I clung to those simple words, as I prayed for the pain to stop. I was so thankful for our dear friends from church who had sent that bouquet to me! I was not really aware of anyone around me, even though I knew Henry might be there, all I could focus on was surviving the horrible pain. This was all new to me. I had always had a very high pain tolerance. I cracked jokes and watched cartoons as I gave birth to our son, too big to pass without forceps, and me refusing any pain medicine. That was a walk in the park! The pain I was having was beyond anything I could comprehend or begin to explain. It was inescapable, all encompassing, white hot searing pain! It seemed to go on forever, except for the brief times right after another injection, that sleep rescued me. As a nurse now, I can look back on it and realize that they had probably snagged my sciatic nerve during surgery. That pain lessened eventually, but stayed with me for over a year, and I spent most of that time, laying on the sofa to avoid flaring it up. Only an anti-inflammatory seemed to give some relief. I gained a lot of weight that year!

I realized later, when I became a nurse, how valuable this trial was. With such a high pain tolerance, I would have trouble understanding other people's pain. Because this happened, I was able to have the compassion and understanding needed for my calling as a nurse. I was grateful for it then! That trial was difficult for me and my family, but we had a bigger trial heading full steam towards us! One of the most difficult trials we have ever been through.

Tares in the Wheat

One night at a home Bible study, our study leader who was an elder with the small local church we had been attending, and some of the others were discussing how upset they were that the pastor was straying from the Scriptures! We were shocked! We remained silent as we listened to what they were saying, and the evidence they listed. These people were quite grounded in the word of God, so we were confused and couldn't wait to leave and try to comprehend what we had just heard! As soon as we got to the car, I opened my Bible study notebook, where I had written all of the sermon notes, and scanned over them for the evidence they had talked about. But in my heart, I knew they were right. There, in black and white, were the pastor's words to us.

The pastor had been invited to attended another church, where the pastor there was taking him under his wing, saying he could lead his church to "success," by following his "Shepherding" example. Our pastor had initiated, a "Shepherding" model, where anyone who wanted to do anything, like buy a car or a home, should meet with one of the "Shepherds", for their guidance! He had been creating "Mediators!" The Scriptures clearly state, "There is One mediator between God and men, the Man Christ Jesus." (I Timothy 2:5) We were annoyed by it, but it hadn't sunk in that what he was doing was against the Scriptures. Then we both recalled, the pastor's last message, where he said that we were not to be praying, "Thy kingdom come!" The blinders had now been removed. Our hearts were broken! We were in a state of shock the next day, and I was crying and asking God for wisdom and direction, when my co-leader in the girl's group at that church called about our meeting. She heard from my voice that I was crying. She asked me what was wrong, and I briefly shared some of what had been revealed to us, asking her to keep it confidential until we could decide our next steps. We never got the chance! She went immediately to the pastor and told him what I had shared. We had been directed by the elder who had exposed those things to us, to wait for him to meet with the pastor and ask him for an explanation. We were shocked when the pastor called us! He was screaming at me, calling me horrible names, but I had such peace. I calmly quoted Scriptures as the Spirit led me, and he could not answer them, he only became angrier and condemning. Then the Lord whispered to my heart, "This is not your pastor." We did not go to services that Sunday, and that was a good thing. The pastor condemned us from the pulpit as "Tares in the wheat," and told the body to never speak with or have contact with us again. Our lives were turned upside down, and we lost every friend we had there. I spent most of the time praying and crying out to God. I couldn't understand why this happened, right when we felt the closest we had ever felt to the Lord and the body of Christ. The pain was made sharper every few days, when the elder who had told us those things, would call me and ask if I had really said such and such, lies the pastor was telling him I had said or done. It was like having the bandage ripped off again and again.

One day, I was in the backyard where I liked to commune with God, complaining to Him about it all. "Why?" I demanded, "I don't understand!" I was desperately pleading with God to tell me why this had to happen. While I paced and debated, I noticed the Boston Fern hanging from the patio cover, choking with dead leaves. I grabbed a pair of scissors out of the kitchen and started whacking away at the poor plant! Then the Lord spoke to my heart and said, "What are you doing?" I knew before I could answer. And with a sigh of relief and thankfulness for His mercy, I responded, "I'm pruning it." Indeed! So many times, in our walks with the Lord, we must be pruned in order to be able to produce more fruit.

> ...and every branch that bears fruit He prunes, that it may bear more fruit. (John 15:2)

We tried going back to our original church, a long drive from us, but it had grown so big, we felt lost and vulnerable. We trusted our old pastor's teaching, but we also needed to be nurtured through what had happened to us. So, for a short time, we turned to a smaller extension of our old church, that was nearby. The kids were adolescents by then and loved the youth group there. We buried ourselves in Bible studies, and although we knew it was not our home church, we understood we were there for a time of healing. It was a healing body, that nurtured wounded people. That spirit of healing became quite tangible shortly after we started attending. I found a lump in my breast. I made an appointment with the doctor, and then went up to the pastor after services and shared what was happening. He prayed with me, for a complete healing. I felt such peace as he prayed for me. I was no longer afraid. They took sonogram images and it took a while to get the results. The doctor had felt the lump, it was there during my visit. But then I got the results from imaging, and there was nothing there! I quickly checked myself, and it was gone! Praise God for His mercy! I am forever grateful for His healing in my life. That was a physical healing, but what I needed most was a spiritual healing. That would be much harder!

I had such anger in my heart for what that other pastor had done to us. I was afraid to run into him in a store, or any of the people we had known. Going anywhere sent me into stealth mode. I did not know how I would respond. Something had to change.

We started attending our old, home church, despite the drive, we knew we were "home," and that the teaching was sound. I joined the women's Bible study and made a friend in my group. I don't make friends easy! I am by nature an introvert. Most people would never guess that. I have a bubbly, outgoing personality, that covers my introversion. My happy chatter keeps people from getting too close. This lady that I was drawn to, and she to me, was my mother's age. She was the picture of health and joy, with a beaming smile, and a depth of wisdom far beyond my own. She was a retired nurse, and that made me feel drawn to her all the more. I had always wanted to be a nurse!

My new friend, Martha, was so encouraging! She was not afraid to tell me when I was off the mark, and would gently correct me. I had been blessed with a true Christian mentor I could look up to. She was so calm when I would call upset about something, and she would give me Bible verses to address whatever I was concerned about, calming me in the process. I was not the happy person I had always been, not after being cast out of that church. I had allowed the poison of unforgiveness to cover me in darkness. I gained weight as I tried to bury my hurt and anger, and I had lost my joy in the Lord, drifting further away from His word and prayer. I was in depression over what had happened. I shared with Martha about the whole thing. She told me I had to give my anger over to the Lord. I didn't know how to do that. I felt I was owed an apology, and I told my husband that. I was shocked at his response! He told me I was the one who should apologize. I was so hurt and felt he was betraying me! Then he read Matthew 5:23-24 to me, reminding me that the Lord would not accept my gift if I had not reconciled with my brother. He was right! I would have to go to him and apologize. I shared this with Martha, and she confirmed what my husband had said. She also said she would be praying for me and that God would give me the words. I needed to humble myself, as I yielded to the Lord's direction.

I struggled for two months trying to get the courage to go, and finally I called and made an appointment. I arrived cheerful, full of the Spirit of the Lord, as He carried me there.

I was shocked when I saw the pastor. He was a young man, but had aged years in that short time. His hair had gone completely white! He looked worn and beaten down. He welcomed me with pleasure, expecting me to apologize, and that did not bother me. I let the Spirit speak, and felt such peace as the words flowed out. He was not touched, but instead he said, "I expect a lot of other people to be coming to apologize!" I was gracious and told him I was praying for him and his wife as I left. It felt as if a giant weight had been lifted from my shoulders. I was free from the darkness of unforgiveness! I had no idea how much it had affected my life, until the weight of it was gone! I was also amazed that it did not concern me that he had not apologized. I had obeyed the Lord, and that was enough. To this day I feel sadness over the hardness of that pastor's heart. I pray he did return to his first love, Jesus. He lost many of his flock, and they were shunned like we were. Through the mercy of God, several of the people we had been such good friends with, who eventually left that church too, invited us to a picnic to be reconciled to each other. It was hard to go, but we knew we should. We felt awkward, but soon our apprehension faded as several of them apologized to us for believing what the pastor had said about us. That was when we learned how they too, had been shunned and maligned from the pulpit. The outcome of it all, ended up being a period of growth spiritually for each of us. Most started fellowshipping at different churches, spreading their gifts and service throughout our area. We all went our separate ways, and I believe that was as God had intended.

> *Therefore those who were scattered went everywhere preaching the word. (Acts 8:4)*

A Troubling Dream

I have always loved my dreams. Always bursting with technicolor, beauty and adventure. It was like going to the movies every night. It had always been that way for me. I loved recounting the crazy stories. But one night, I had a dream that was horrible and shocking. I dreamt that our son had been molested, and what was so upsetting to me, was how calm I was in the dream, unshaken and not seeking revenge! I woke up crying and disgusted with my inaction, and I prayed that God would take the memory of that awful dream away. I fell back asleep, and was back in the same dream! Only this time I was sharing the Lord with those who had molested my son. I woke up immediately in furious anger, screaming, "No, No, I won't share the Lord! Let them burn! Let them burn after what they did to my son, my only son!" As those last three words came out of my mouth, God reminded me how He had sacrificed His only Son, so that He might forgive us through the spilling of His Son's precious blood, and rescue us from the sin that would destroy us, His children, those who would accept His free gift of salvation through Christ Jesus.

For God so loved the world that He gave His only begotten Son, that whoever believes in Him should not perish but have everlasting life. (John 3:16)

Little did I know, that the dream was not just for me to understand how much God loves and forgives us. It also revealed a truth that had not yet come to light.

Our Home

We were happy in our home, but knew that we might receive a call from the owner wanting to sell it one day; and that call came in the summer, as I had a group of ladies in my home for a houseware party. I miss those parties! The call was from the owner, and he told me that he wanted to sell the house, but that he liked us, so he was offering it to us first! I told him I would relay the message to Henry, and I was really worried, knowing we did not have a down payment for a house. When I told Henry, he was upset too, not knowing what we should do. I was so proud of Henry, as he went to see a pastor at our home church, asking for prayer. The pastor told him that maybe this was an open door from the Lord, but to continue praying for guidance from the Lord. After we checked the prices to rent another place, and realized they were all way too expensive for us, Henry asked his folks if they would be able to give us a loan for the down payment, and they agreed. We were so thankful and joyous over this blessing from the Lord! Unfortunately, things did not go so easy. The loan companies were not helpful, were treating us badly, and escrow was taking months instead of weeks. Then Henry's Teamster Local went on strike! Everything came to a halt, and the loan sat without any progress through November and December. We had entered escrow in August! Henry was working side jobs to keep food on the table while the strike lingered on, and the owner who had been so patient and kind, finally decided to put our home on the open market! I will never forget the day they put a "For Sale" sign in our front yard! We had people walking through our home as we held our breath and stifled our tears.

Finally, the strike was over! The escrow wheels started grinding again, slowly, and we waited. We had decided as soon as we had entered escrow, to have a Bible study in our home as a way of dedicating it to God. Henry did not wait, and we welcomed new friends to our home for the first Bible study in February. I remember their confusion when they saw the "For Sale" sign. But we were trusting Jesus, hanging on to the hope that our home would truly be ours. Finally, in April, nine months after entering escrow, the house was ours! It wasn't until then that we understood why the Lord had allowed such a long delay! When we had entered escrow back in August, the interest rate was sixteen percent. When we closed, it was eight percent! The Lord, had been merciful to us. What a blessing! What a gift! We were so humbled by His grace towards us.

> *And we know that all things work together for good to those who love God, to those who are called according to His purpose. (Romans 8:28)*

During that year and the next, we made good friends at our home church, in our neighborhood, in Scouts and in our home Bible study. Our kids were doing well, active in school, church and Scouts, and our son was thriving in BMX. Our lives were busy and happy.

A Gift

I loved the Women's Ministry, led by the pastor's wife at our home church. I also loved the different events they held, like the Mother & Daughter Tea, and especially the retreats. I was eager to go to the Spring Retreat coming up. I went by myself, and they had shared rooms. There were two other ladies in my room, and they were friends, so I was free to go by myself to the studies that interested me. I was curious about a class called Spiritual Gifts, and decided to go. I had heard others pray in the spirit, usually quietly, during group prayer. It fascinated me, but I really didn't think it was a gift I needed. I thought that because I was always able to verbalize my feelings, I did not need that gift. I didn't really understand what the gift of tongues was all about. I was about to learn! The class was very educational, and I learned that the gift of tongues, was for speaking to God through the Spirit; unless there is an interpreter, to translate a message from the Lord to the body (church). Otherwise, our "tongue" or prayer language was for our private worship and prayer time with the Lord. (See 1 Corinthians 14) Then they asked those who wanted to receive the gift of tongues, to stay and be prayed for by some of the women leaders. I am very private when it comes to something like that, but I was too embarrassed to just leave, and felt that maybe I should stay and be prayed for. A very kind older lady laid hands on me and prayed for me, and despite my embarrassment, I felt a strange sensation in my throat. It was as if something was stuck in my throat, and I had to let it out! I could not do that there. I excused myself, quickly left and ran to my room, hoping and praying my roommates would not be there. Praise God, the room was empty! I sat on the bed and prayed for the Lord to guide and help me, but I could not figure out how to release it out of my mouth. One of the leaders had said, to just start making a sound, and it would come out. I tried, and it wasn't until I sang a tune, that it burst forth in the most beautiful song! I did not know the language, but it was lilting and beautiful. It sounded to me like the voices of women singing praise to God in Israel. I had never experienced anything like it. It took my breath, and I found myself gasping for air. It flowed out like a river, and I had to consciously take breaths in. It took a while to learn how to breath as I spoke in tongues! That day, which was the day I would be driving home, down from the mountain top, was a day I will always remember! I couldn't wait to get in my car, and I let the Spirit pour out the songs of praise to God all the way home. I don't often sing in the spirit; I usually just pray in my prayer language privately. I do sing in the spirit, when my heart is bursting with the joy of the Lord! It was a few years later, as I listened to the words I was praying, that I recognized the word, "Adonai" (the name of God in Hebrew), and realized my prayer language was in Hebrew. No wonder that first experience sounded to me like Israeli women singing praises to God!

I only share this because it was a pivotal time in my life, where prayer would be so very important. I don't talk about my prayer language, or use it in public. I do not speak Hebrew, so I cannot interpret, and I have never felt led by God to pray in the spirit during a gathering of believers, where there may be an interpreter. I'm sure that if God wanted to share a message with the body while I was present, He would prompt me to speak in my prayer language, and He would also provide someone to interpret.

If anyone speaks in a tongue, let there be two or at the most three, each in turn, and let one interpret. But if there is no interpreter, let him keep silent in church, and let him speak to himself and to God. For God is not the author of confusion but of peace, as in all the churches of the saints. (1 Corinthians 14:27,28 & 33)

Forgiving Myself

That same year, I was listening to Christian radio, and enjoying a daily Christian family program. One week they did a series on healing from abortion. I had buried that part of my past away, and had not dealt with my guilt about it. My abortion, although at the time I really wanted it, ended up being one of the most horrible events of my life.

As I revealed earlier about my youth, I was quite promiscuous, and when I realize I was pregnant just after my 17th birthday, I had no idea who the father was! The men I had been with, were all 21 or older, and when I told them, a few left the states. It didn't matter to me; I just wanted my pregnancy over with! After all, it was just tissue. That is what everyone said, and I believed it; I needed to believe it! I tried to end the pregnancy myself, but was unsuccessful, so finally I went in for an illegal abortion. They would be legalized a short time later, but I found a doctor who was running a clinic just for that purpose. When I went in, it was packed with girls my age, tearful and sobbing. I thought, *"Why are you crying? You're getting the problem taken care of!"* Still, it frightened me, as I saw girls coming out from the back of the clinic crying. Surely this won't hurt, I thought. I was wrong. The sedation they gave me did nothing for the pain. And the procedure was a failure. I was sent home to miscarry. I believe that happened for a reason; so that I would be able to see my baby. To know that he was a real baby, not just tissue. To see his little fingers and toes. Most women are kept from seeing the result of their "choice." They can pretend it never happened. I could never forget, or forgive myself for what I had done. After I had accepted Christ, I logically believed that Jesus had forgiven me *all* my sins. Yet in my heart, I could not believe He would ever, could ever, forgive such a thing! After the births of my daughter and son, I realized the gift of His mercy and grace. But I still felt so unworthy. I could not forgive myself. I was hesitant to listen to the program, but was drawn in quickly by the loving way they addressed the women who had lost their children to abortion. I didn't know that any Christian would forgive us. The program led us to seek God through prayer, and to ask God to give us a name for our child, to help us grieve the loss of our children. I prayed fervently, and the Lord, in His great mercy, gave me his name, "Timothy." It means, honoring God. I realized he was giving honor to God in His presence. Then, the Lord gave me a vision of Him! Full grown, in his perfected body, beautiful to behold! He was tall, with a mass of curly blond hair. What a blessing it was to see him! The Lord is *so* merciful! The vision also revealed who the father was; he was the very image of the man, only perfect! I was *so* very thankful for that radio program! I wrote them and let them know. I also yearned to hold an image of my baby son, and found a company that produced small plastic babies, the size of an 11-12 weeks gestation baby. They used a model of a baby boy, to show the development at that stage. I ordered one, and it came with an information card, telling about the growth of the baby. It seemed to be an important step for me, to have a replica of my child. I waited eagerly for it to arrive, and when it came, I made a little bunting out of a piece of soft quilt, to cover him. I carried that little baby in my pocket, or my purse for over a year. I just wanted to be close to him. I was finally understanding God's merciful forgiveness towards me.

That abortion is the only thing I have done that I wish I could undo. It was a tragedy in my life; damaging my heart, my body and my spirit, as well as ending the life of my child. I am so thankful that the Lord has cast my sins into the depths of the sea!

> *He will again have compassion on us,*
> *And will subdue our iniquities.*
> *You will cast all our sins*
> *Into the depths of the sea. (Micah 7:19)*

A Mysterious Dream

The following year I had a strange dream. I knew that this dream was from the Lord, but I did not know the interpretation.

I dreamt that I was wearing an amethyst bracelet, with a cluster of raw amethyst stones going around my wrist. I knew in the dream, that my mother had given me the bracelet. Then I took off the bracelet and went to hand it to her, and surprised, she said, "You're not giving it back to me, are you?" Then I responded, "Not really." And I took a stone from the bracelet and gave it to her, saying, "Take this as a stone of remembrance of me." I awoke with the words, "stone of remembrance," still on my lips. When it was morning, I could think of nothing else! I tried to find "stone of remembrance" in the Bible, but could not, even using our good Strong's Concordance. When Henry got home (He still worked nights then), I told him about the dream, and asked where I might find it in the bible, and he told me in Joshua, chapter 4, verse 7. The translation was "memorial stones", that's why I couldn't find it. (So thankful we have Bible applications now!) When I read the passage, I did not see a connection to my dream. I felt compelled to find the interpretation. I prayed, asking God to reveal the dream to me, and He did! The bracelet represented my life, and each stone was a year of my life. The bracelet had been given to me by my mother, as she had given birth to me. I was born in February, with the amethyst as my birthstone. It was so clearly the perfect interpretation. But I was still confused. Why did I give a stone, one year of my life, to my mother? What did that mean? I asked the Lord, "Am I going to die?" But I thought, "No, I only gave her one stone, not the whole bracelet." The dream consumed my thoughts for a long time, and I sought counsel from church, still with no answer. I decided that God would reveal it to me in His time, and tried to put it out of my mind. But the enemy was sitting there on my shoulders, whispering fearful thoughts! I really thought it meant that I would die in a year. The father of lies was turning what should have been a blessing for me, into a point of fear. I withdrew, I became depressed, I gained more weight, I stopped reading the bible, and I stopped praying!

Almost a year later, I went to church to ask a pastor about the dream, and he did not have an answer. I went to the women's Bible study a few minutes later, and a woman got up to give her testimony of God's work in her life. Then she quoted a verse, that I knew God wanted me to hear!

> Then the LORD answered me and said:
> "Write the vision
> And make it plain on tablets,
> That he may run who reads it.
> For the vision is yet for an appointed time;
> But at the end it will speak, and it will not lie.
> Though it tarries, wait for it;
> Because it will surely come,
> It will not tarry. (Habakkuk 2:2-3)

I knew the Lord was speaking to me! So I wrote it all down, and I waited; for my death. The enemy had so thoroughly convinced me that I was going to die, that I could not see passed it! The Lord had just given me encouragement! But I took it as thinking my fate was sealed, and it was only a matter of time.

Journal entries I made during that time, reflected my thankfulness for the way the Lord seemed to cover me with His peace whenever I prayed in the spirit. It was a deep connection to the Lord, that carried me through that time. The Lord kept me close to Him, as we went through all the trials and issues facing us.

My Precious Grandma

Time was catching-up to my precious grandma, and her health started to decline.

I loved my grandma! I spent a lot of time with her and grandpa on their chicken farm as a little girl. It was a place of simple pleasures, safety and love. Grandma was a Southern farm girl, transplanted west when her mom was ill, and the doctor told her dad to move to a fresher climate. Grandma was in her teens then.

I have such wonderful memories of her. I remember so clearly the sweet smell of her hankie, with traces of Evening in Paris, as she would lick it and wipe my face. I loved her smiling face and giggles. She was so gracious and a delight to be around. But she was also really down to earth, and could take care of herself, her loved ones, and make a mean pot of chicken and "dumplins!"

At first, we did not recognize that she was having mini-strokes. The first sign was when she "fell" at our annual family picnic. She didn't complain of much pain, but her hip was red and hot to the touch, so we put a cold compress on it and had her rest. Henry and I decided we better take her in to be seen, and she had broken her hip! After a brief stay in the hospital, they gave her a walker and encouraged her to walk, because it was a hairline fracture. They felt it would heal well, and said she had the bones of a thirty-year old! They were right! She was doing her exercises faithfully, and healed quickly. But there were also problems with her memory. She was forgetting to pay some bills, and had over paid others! My uncle started going to her apartment every month to pay her bills for her and to manage her finances. My mom and dad had moved north, so her care was up to me. Soon she started needing personal care, help with bathing, and house cleaning. I was going to her apartment, where she still lived alone, to help her several days a week. As the weeks and months passed, she needed more help. One night, as Henry was driving me home after helping her bathe, he said we needed to think about moving her in with us. I was so thankful that he offered that, before I needed to ask! Henry loved her too. She was his grandma all through our marriage. His grandma had died when he was young, and he loved my grandma's happy, sweet nature. Our daughter had married and left earlier that year, so we had a spare room. We were almost finished painting it, and had purchased a new, guest bed. Only a couple of days after Henry told me to think about bringing grandma home, she called me, telling me she had fallen and couldn't get up. I raced to her apartment, and found her sitting in her chair, a big lump on her forehead. I went to the kitchen to get a cold compress, and saw a pot on the stove, flame on high, and the water burned down. I turned off the flame, and returned with a cold compress. I gently soothed her forehead, and told her she needed to come home with me. She surprised me when she calmly said, "Okay." She had been on her own for a while, outliving her last husband. She had always been so self-sufficient, walking to the grocery store and the Senior Center. Now she was understanding that she could not make it on her own, and with the graciousness that was her hallmark, she accepted her fate.

We made her room as familiar and cozy as possible, bringing her dresser, television, and some of her favorite things. We had a rocker in her room too. But she liked spending time with us the best. We had always taken her with us when we went to fun places, and she was already such a big part of our lives, moving her in with us was a natural choice. I was not working, having quit the job I took at an office supply store earlier that year, after paying for our daughter's wedding. My mother came down to visit, and my uncles too, all of them thanking me for taking her in. It was early November, just before the busy holiday season. I was happy to be able to include her in it all.

Caring for grandma was hard and heartbreaking. She was declining daily, getting more confused and having episodes of paranoia, where she thought she heard or saw things that were not there. Her incontinence was increasing, and that involved much more work. But I felt nothing but love and compassion for her, when I was caring for her. I was encouraged during her times of clarity, when she would share with me what her life was like as a girl in the southern plains. She told me about when her baby brother died, at only 2 years old, and losing a sister, only 12 years old to diabetes. She also told me about not having a refrigerator, and how they kept a wet piece of leather draped over a small tent-like frame on the porch, where they kept their cheese and milk. She also told me in detail, how at church, she felt as if someone was pulling her to go down the aisle and accept Christ, and she finally gave in, and went down on her own. I loved hearing all about her and her family, and learned so much from her!

The following January, grandma had a mini-stroke and was hospitalized for 2 weeks. The first week, I missed her and wanted her back. The second week, I started enjoying free time with Henry and our son, Gabriel. I became apprehensive about having her return. But the Lord made it clear that He wanted me to care for her. My mom came down to be with her in the hospital, and I really enjoyed her company! Mom was so very appreciative for my care of grandma. She said it meant so much to her, and that she felt so bad about not being able to do it herself. She also said several times, that I was her hand extended. Grandma came home while Mom was here, and she really enjoyed spending time with her. Mom had to go home, and was heartbroken to leave her. Grandma's dementia was increasing, along with delusions and incontinence, making it very hard for me to care for her. I didn't know if I could take it much longer, when our daughter, Claire called me, and read 2 Corinthians 12:9-10 to me.

"And He said to me, 'My grace is sufficient for you, for My strength is made perfect in weakness.' Therefore most gladly I will rather boast in my infirmities, that the power of Christ may rest upon me."

Then one evening, while relaxing with Henry, God revealed the dream from six years before to me. The amethyst I gave my mother, was the year I would spend caring for her mother, my precious grandma! The prophecy was being fulfilled! When I realized that I was caring for my grandma as a gift for my mother, I rejoiced in the love and mercy of God! I realized that caring for her was an honor, not a task, but a holy privilege. It gave me the encouragement I needed to continue to serve her and my Lord with a joyous heart. Henry was also greatly relieved. He had been quite worried about me, but understanding the plan God had laid out long before any of it had happened, gave him and me such peace, knowing God had it all in His hands!

Several months later, Grandma had a bad stroke. I went in to wake her, and her eyes were opened, filled with fear, but she could not move or speak. Her lower abdomen was swollen taut and hot. I called 911, and they took her away to the hospital. I felt like a lost child! I followed them to the hospital, and called my mom and uncles. The doctor felt she was sinking fast, her kidneys had shut down, and said her family needed to come right away. Mom, and all my uncles arrived, and I was standing meekly in the background, as the decision was made to move her to a Care Home, because they did not think she would last long. I felt helpless, and stripped of my connection to her, after all, I was just the granddaughter. I stood, listening to the doctor telling them that she would not want them to try and prolong her life with forced feedings, and they all agreed. I was thankful for that! Her doctor knew her very well. She really liked him too. I wanted her to come back home with me, but the decision was taken away from me. I was hurt, and crying. Momma sat down with me in the cavernous lobby, and I wanted to run away. I told her through tears, that I wanted Grandma to come home with me! And with the gentleness of an angel, Momma said to me, "Hannah, you don't realize how hard you've been working. You need a rest." I knew she meant well, but I was so heartbroken to think of losing her. It was only a few days later, that I recognized how right my momma was! I was extremely exhausted! Momma stayed in town for a month, because we all thought Grandma would be dying soon, but she got a bit better, and stabilized. She was always pretty tough! We made frequent visits, and she could recognize us sometimes, and say a few words. She would always smile when she saw me. Momma went back home, and my uncles and I continued to make frequent visits.

My Birth Father

During that time, I had been thinking a lot about my birth father. God had led me to pray for him over the past year, and I felt God wanted me to be reconciled to him. I had not seen him since I was 4 years old. There was a good reason for that.

My momma was just sixteen years old when my father, on a two week leave from Korea, asked her to marry him. He was head over heels in love, but Momma did not love him. She told me that she just didn't know how to tell him no, as he looked at her with pleading eyes, so she said, "Yes." She knew she had made a mistake, but could not speak up and tell him so. They were quickly married at the courthouse with her parents, and his parents there. She cried, and they all thought she was crying because she was happy, but it was because she knew she was making a mistake. They had a short time together before he had to go back to Korea, and so shy and regretful, she only let him near her once. He returned to Korea, and a short time later, she realized she was pregnant. It gave her the determination to stand up for herself, and she wrote him a "Dear John" letter. He was devastated, writing her back and telling her how heartbroken he was. But Mom stood her ground, and got a job to support us both. My father married another young girl, and started a family. I was raised mostly on Grandma and Grandpa's chicken farm, so they could watch me while Momma worked and dated.

I must have been about three years old, when Momma found out she was pregnant, and her boyfriend left her. I was sixteen when Momma told me all about what had happened to her, in an effort to keep me from having sex with my boyfriend. It broke my heart to hear her recount it, but I was too stubborn to learn from her example. She told me she found a haven in the Salvation Army, and they had a retreat for unwed mothers in the mountains. She said they were all so wonderful to her and the other girls, that they all felt like treasured daughters. She said it was one of the best times she ever had. She gave birth to a baby boy, and she named him, and nursed him for three weeks, hoping to keep him. She soon realized that she would never be able to support two children on her meager income, so she decided to give him up for adoption. The Salvation Army helped her and stood by her through that whole process. She never forgot all they did for her, and always donated to them instead of any other charity. She longed to find him some day, and left her information in case he ever wanted to find her. I hope one day we will be reunited, hopefully through my DNA.

I was staying with Grandma and Grandpa, while she was away for his birth, and I only have wonderful memories of my time with them. I loved wandering around their small home and chicken farm, the old porch swing, the shed where I found a box of old paper dolls, the big Fig Tree where I made mud pies with my cousins, and especially the pantry where they had the incubator for the baby chicks! I loved to pet their downy soft little bodies. I loved being there, except for the old rooster, who must have thought I was another rooster with my red hair, and attacked me several times before grandma had enough and told grandpa to kill him. I remember clearly, watching grandpa as he performed the grim task. I remember happily watching grandma clean and pluck him in the sink, and grandma said he was the toughest bird they ever ate, but Hannah happily ate every bite on her plate! How I loved my grandma and grandpa!

Then, just after my fourth birthday, my world came crashing down.

I Want My Momma!

A terrible thing had happened to my momma! She had a friend that she visited every now and then, and apparently, someone else who lived there had been selling drugs. On one of her visits there, the police raided the house, and Momma was arrested, along with others in the house, and she was sent to jail to wait for her day in court. I went to stay with my uncle and his family, but not for long. The local newspaper reported the arrest, and when my birth father read it, he went to my uncle's house and took me away with him. He and his young wife had a baby, and another would soon be on the way. He had taken her far away from her family farm, to where he lived. She had no family in town, and my father's family did not accept her. His parents were Catholic, and wanted him to get back with my mom, because they were upset about him getting a divorce. And my father often slipped and called her by my mother's name. I can't image how she must have felt, and then, having the daughter of her husband's first love brought home for her to care for. I was a perky, happy child; everyone said I was a good, obedient little girl. Then, I found myself in a strange place, without those I loved. I felt alone and frightened. I wanted my momma! Momma said they only brought me to see her in jail twice in the six months while she was waiting for her trial to come to court. The first time, she could see me at the bottom of a very long stairwell, and seeing her, I cried out "Momma! Momma!" but there had been a riot, so they wouldn't let us visit. The second time, I was in a trance like state, and called her by her given name, as instructed by my father, who threatened me on the way there. That visit devastated my poor mother! She had a girlfriend who lived near my father. She told my momma that I was not acting like myself; I did not recognize her, didn't speak and seemed to be in a daze.

However, God provided a place of sanctuary for me during that time. My momma had insisted that they let me go to church, and her friend, along with her family would pick me up on Sundays, and take me to their gospel church. I *loved* church! I felt loved, safe and happy. I loved it when the Sunday

School teachers took us into the sanctuary to sing along with the congregation. I loved seeing the ladies all dressed up for church, raising their hands in joyful praise to the Lord! I remember, "This Little Light of Mine", "Jesus Loves Me" and "The Wise Man Built His House Upon the Rock"! I also remember looking forward to getting a stick of gum as we left. Sometimes Juicy Fruit, sometimes Double-mint, I still love them to this day.

But I also remembered two other things from that time. We went on a trip to the zoo, with my father and step-mother, and their baby in a stroller. We were looking at an alligator enclosure, in a shady, secluded part of the zoo, with vines growing on the fence. My father picked me up with a jerk, and dangled me by one foot over the enclosure. I remember being terrified, but I did not respond. I think maybe that is why he did it, to elicit a response of some kind. But I would not react!

I also remembered, there was a fight between my father and step-mother, and my father took me out of their one-story apartment in the night, and carried me to the back of the building, between the building and the back fence, where there was a narrow strip filled with ivy. He set me down in the far corner, and told me not to move. "There are man-eating rats in the ivy, so you had better not move or make a sound, or they will find you and eat you." He said to me. I remember so clearly, whimpering, trying not to make any noise as I wept, fearful of any movement in the ivy. It seemed like a very long time, when, out of the darkness, I heard a familiar voice, it was my uncle! He had come to check on me, and they did not answer the door as he heard them arguing. But he also heard me! He followed my little, crying voice, and found me in the ivy, in the cold, dark night. I know my uncle well, and I'm sure tempers were flaring that night. But he couldn't legally take me, so I remained with them until Momma's case came to court. They threw out her conviction and set her free. The bailiff said to her as she left the courtroom, "See you next time." And with the firmness of a determined woman, she said, "There won't be a 'next time!'" Momma was standing on her own two feet, and she would never go back! She got custody of me easily, especially after the judge saw that due to the abuse, I had lost a large portion of my hair, a bald spot covering the crown of my head. She took me to a court appointed Child Psychologist, and apparently many things came out at the sessions, because the last thing she told my momma, was that I was to never see my father again. I am so grateful for the wisdom of my mother in never speaking ill of my father. She always told me, "I know your father loved you." I never heard a bad thing from her about him. That was a blessing! She married my "Daddy" (stepfather) a few years later; a gentle, soft-spoken man, and finally, I was part of a loving, happy family!

Reconciliation

Henry knew I had been wanting to reconnect with my birth father, despite the memories I had. My mom always told me not to judge others for what they do, because you never know what might have caused them to do it. I held no anger towards my father or his wife. All I knew was that God clearly wanted me to pray for them and be reconciled. One day, Henry came home with news of an organization he heard about on the radio, that could find anyone in the USA, just from their name! I really got excited, because my birth father's name was so unusual! So, the next day I called the number, and within a minute, they had his address and phone number! It was the beginning of the computer generation, and I was very grateful! I thought it would be much better to write him a letter, rather than call him. I didn't know if my call would be accepted. So I made a picture collage, showing my life and our children, and I wrote him a long letter. I began with the words, "First I want you to know that my mom never said anything bad about you, and always told me that she knew you loved me." I also included my testimony, telling him about the importance of Jesus Christ in my life, and I prayed over that letter, and sent it off. A few days later, I returned home to find a message on our recorder, "Hello, Hannah? This is your father, I'd really like to talk to you, I love you." I screamed and danced and rejoiced, crying with joy and thankfulness! I called him back, and we talked for a good long time. He lived in an area not too far from where my momma and daddy lived. We had already planned to go and visit Momma and Daddy in October, so we decided to go and see him and his family after we visited them. I was so excited! Then a few days later, I received a letter from my half-sibling. Included were pictures of their family, and my father! Then they wrote, "We always knew we had an older sister." I can't express how thankful and happy I was, to know that they had not kept me a secret! They told their children about me! I was eager to meet them all, but concerned about his wife. I was fearful she would not be happy about all of this, and would not be receptive.

Before I knew it, we were on our way! My visit with Momma and Daddy was sweet and tender, but Momma expressed concern about my visit with them. "They owe you an apology." She said. I told her, "I know, but I have a great sense of peace about it Momma, so I know God will work it out." It was a long drive, reaching their house in the early evening. My father was outside waiting, and rushed to my door, hugging me so tight when I got out of the car. All reservations fell away! As we entered the house, there sitting meekly knitting, was his wife. I could tell in an instant that she was a gentle, kind spirit. She smiled, warmly greeting me, and I hugged her, surprising her. She was so shy! But she told us how excited and happy my father was when he got my letter! He shared with me, that he had tried to reconnect with his own birth father, and when he reached him, he rejected him, saying, "I don't have a son." Then he said that he was afraid to try and find me, fearful I would reject him, too. Tears were forming in his eyes, as he expressed how thankful he was that I had found him.

I had brought a photo album with photos of our kids through the years, including our daughter's wedding. It was a joyous, happy reunion! They had prepared a room upstairs for us to spend the night. It was so hard to sleep! I was giddy with excitement! I got up very early the next morning, and went into the kitchen, where my step-mother was making coffee and preparing for the day. I chattered happily, telling stories about our kids, when she put her head down, and quietly said, "I thought you would hate me." I replied, "Why would I hate you?" Then she said, "I was a wicked step-mother to you." I replied, "I know, I remember, but I have no right not to forgive anyone, because Jesus forgave me all of my sins." And I told her that I understood, but she said she didn't understand how I could. I reassured her that I had always understood, and couldn't imagine how difficult it must have been for her then. Then I told her I forgave her. I was surprised when she shared with me, that they had another child, the youngest, who died in a traffic accident a few years before. (That was the same year that the Lord had led me to pray for my father!) She said she felt it was punishment from God for the way she had treated me! "No!" I said, telling her that God doesn't work like that. It was simply their time to go, and had nothing to do with her past mistakes. I told her about the all-encompassing love and forgiveness of Christ, and that He loved her, as I tried to comfort her. She had lived with the burden of guilt for so many years! I realized that the Lord had led me to be reconciled, not just for my father, but for her! She said I had taken a tremendous burden off of her shoulders. She went to the kitchen wall, where she had a beautiful collection of plates on the wall, and she brought down a plate, that had the depiction of the Last Supper on it. She said that they received it as a gift when they were married, and she said she wanted me to have it. It is currently displayed proudly in my china cabinet. Then that same day, I met my half-siblings, and later I sat at the table poking and touching the face and hands of my father. I have his ears and his hands. He was beaming, so happy, such a sweet, kind man. I was also happy to see how much he loved his wife. The gleam in his eyes when he looked at her was unmistakable. We took pictures together, and then we said our good-byes. I couldn't wait to get to a phone booth and call my momma! I told her all about what my stepmother said, and Momma was really touched. She said, "Oh the poor woman!" Momma and I both had a heart for her, and Momma was very happy for me.

Grandma Goes Home

Soon it was Thanksgiving. It was so hard to have Thanksgiving without my grandma! But I refused to let her miss out on her very favorite Thanksgiving treat, Mincemeat Pie! She was the only one in the family who liked it, but Mom had always made one for her. So, I bought a Mincemeat Pie, and after dinner, I heated it up and drove to the Care Home, and asked the nurses if I could please give just a little bite to Grandma, and told them how much she loved it. She had been choking, so she was on NPO, which means, nothing by mouth. But the nurses, in their mercy, told me okay, just a little bit. I gave them the rest of the pie for the other residents, and they were grateful, saying that many there had asked for it. I took a little piece, and went in to see her. She smiled, but did not speak, and I told her that I had a bit of Mincemeat Pie, and her eyes lit up! I put a tiny bite into her mouth, and I will never forget the look of joy on her face! She slowly chewed, relishing the taste, and swallowed fine. I tried hard to keep from bursting into tears, and gratefully she fell fast asleep. I ran out, blubbering like a baby, crying out to the nurses at the nurse's station, "Thank you so much!" as I raced past them for the safety of my car, where I cried and cried.

In late January, I felt led to share Revelation 7:16–17 with Grandma. Grandma was close to dying and Momma had flown down and was with her. Momma called to tell me she was slipping away, and to come right away. When I arrived, Grandma was lucid enough for me to tell her how much we all loved her. I stayed with her all day, and was able to tell her that she was going to be with Jesus soon, and she would see her mom and dad and her little brother, and it would be wonderful! Then I read those verses to her.

> They shall neither hunger anymore nor thirst anymore; the sun shall not strike them, nor any heat; for the Lamb who is in the midst of the throne will shepherd them and lead them to living fountains

of waters. And God will wipe away every tear from their eyes. (Revelation 7:16–17)

It was the day before my birthday, when I got the call. Grandma was quite close to passing. Momma called me in tears to tell me. My uncles had come and visited her that day, but it was just Momma and Uncle Ted with her when she called. She asked me if I wanted to come and be with Grandma, but I really felt it was important for her and Uncle Ted to have that private time with her, so I said no.

Grandma was hanging on longer than they thought, and the nurse asked if there was something that was left unfinished in her life. Momma realized that Grandma had a secret in her past, that she felt bad about, and although her kids knew about it, it was never discussed. Grandma needed to be forgiven. So, Momma told her she knew about it, and she told her she forgave her. Grandma's breathing relaxed, and she started to slip away.

Momma was so worried that Grandma would die on my birthday; I was too, but I trusted that God knew what He was doing. Right after Momma called, a dear neighbor friend of our daughter's and ours, Suzy, called me to thank me for giving her a Bible, and I told her what was happening. She told me, "Oh, don't worry Hannah, she will be your angel in heaven!" That really touched my heart, and I knew God was comforting me. A minute or two later, Momma called again, crying, to tell me

Grandma had passed. But she also told me, that the moment she took her last breath, she lit up as if someone had turned the light on! She looked to see if the light was on, but it wasn't! She said grandma was glowing, and then, it slowly faded away. My momma needed to see that! She needed the reassurance that grandma was at peace, in the arms of Jesus. God had comforted my momma, too!

> *Precious in the sight of the Lord, is the death of His saints. (Psalm 116:15)*

Then the next day, on my birthday, I got a card in the mail from my birth father, and inside the card, was a small angel pin, with a tiny amethyst on it! He did not know about what had happened with Grandma, or the dream with the amethyst bracelet! And yet, the Lord in His mercy, prompted him to buy that little pin and send it to me. I cried bittersweet tears, over the loss of my grandma, but mostly over the amazing, merciful grace of my Savior! He is my Comforter!

> *Blessed are those who mourn,*
> *For they shall be comforted.*
> *(Jesus tells us, in Matthew 5:4)*

Why, God?

It wasn't long after Grandma went home to Jesus, that my daughter broke down and finally told me that she had been molested, not by one person, but by several during her childhood. I was shocked and so angry! My husband and I did everything possible to keep her safe. We were accused of being over-protective by all who knew us. I was so afraid of that very thing! How could God have allowed that? I tried my best to comfort my daughter, but I could hardly see for the anger I felt towards God. It was a horrible feeling, to be angry with God. I was shaken to my core, and felt distant from Him, and I knew it could not continue. I had to go before the throne. I went into my room, and poured out my heart to God. I cried hard, sobbing on my bed in anguish. "Why?" I asked; "Why did this have to happen?" I was crying and praying for some time before God showed me a vision. It was a beautiful vessel, and it had an intricate design being etched into it, but it was unfinished, with a rough surface. And the Lord whispered to me, "I am making a vessel of your daughter." My anger melted away, and I received what the Lord had said to me.

> *But we have this treasure in earthen vessels, that the excellence of the power may be of God and not of us. (2 Corinthians 4:7)*

I had asked the Lord many times, for my children to be people who would make a difference in the world, not to just slide through life. I wanted them to be servants of God. Being a servant only happens through the trials and troubles we face in this life. It is those things that polish us into the gems Christ created us to be; able to help and encourage others who have suffered as we have.

> *Blessed be the God and Father of our Lord Jesus Christ, the Father of mercies and God of all comfort, who comforts us in all our tribulation, that we may be able*

> *to comfort those who are in any trouble, with the comfort with which we ourselves are comforted by God. (2 Corinthians 1:3–4)*

God's merciful answer to me, helped me be able to tell my poor husband, the one who had always been the fierce protector of his children. He was devastated, and felt so helpless, not being able to punish those responsible.

Not long after that, we discovered that our son, "my only son", had suffered molestation also. I recalled the dream that God had given me several years before that. What I had dreaded, became real. Only, like our daughter, there wasn't a way to punish the perpetrators. Like many children who are abused, their minds blocked out the details, just like I did. We were thrown into a whirlwind of heartache, broken-hearted over the violation of our children, and the burden they were carrying.

I am so very grateful, that today both of our children, now middle-aged, are using the gifts God has given them, to be beautiful vessels of the Lord. I'm sure God isn't finished with them, or any of us, until we are with Him, in heaven.

> *... he will be a vessel for honor, sanctified and useful for the Master, prepared for every good work. (2 Timothy 2:21)*

A New Calling

As our son reached the age of eighteen, my desire to become a nurse was growing stronger, and I felt God leading me to go to college. My friendship with Martha, who often spoke of her love of nursing, gave me the confidence to finally, consider going to college. But the idea of leaving my cozy home made me fearful. I loved my role as full time wife and mother for the past 20 plus, years. I was actually hoping my son would tell me I needed to stay home, so I would not have to step out. So, I asked him what he thought, about me going to college to become a Registered Nurse. I was surprised by his answer! He smiled and said, "Ma, you need to quit worrying about us and get on with your life." There went the excuse I was hoping for! Now, I no longer had the "kids" as an excuse for keeping me from pursuing my lifelong dream.

When I was about 5 years old, I had to go to the hospital to have my tonsils removed. There was a wonderful, encouraging nurse, who took me on a tour of the hospital, showing me the different areas and patients. I was amazed and loved everything she showed me. I had no fear as I was wheeled into surgery, because she walked along side me the whole way, holding my hand. I was fascinated by all of the equipment, and the doctors with masks on. I dreamed during surgery, that the doctor used one of those long plastic teaspoons, popular at the time, to scoop out my tonsils! I loved being in the hospital, getting ice cream to soothe my throat, and being cared for by the sweet nurse all dressed in white. She became my heroine, and lifelong goal. I wanted to be just like her! I began my nursing career on my dolls! They all had scars from imaginary surgeries, etched into their plastic bodies with a sewing needle. My momma was not comfortable with nursing type duties, so I always volunteered to take care of my younger brother and sister's wounds. I was also calm and collected enough to bury the dead pets. It just came naturally to me. As a mother, Gabriel afforded me an internship, of sorts, in Emergency Nursing, with his frequent injuries. I always felt so thankful to be able to help my children when they were sick or injured. I also felt led to rush to the aid of folks involved in accidents near me. Nothing I saw seemed to bother me, as I was able to calm and help them. I was always meant to be a nurse.

With the amazing support of my husband, who had been telling me for years, to go ahead and pursue my dream of nursing, the support of my family, along with the guidance and encouraging words of my friend Martha, I was quickly on my way to a Registered Nursing career! It was not an easy task! I burdened myself with the goal of perfection, that had me exhausted and wanting to give up and quit many times! But Martha and Henry would not allow me to "throw in the towel."

The most difficult trial for me in nursing school, was when I made a mistake. It was in my Pediatrics rotation, caring for an infant. I had used the formula the nurse had told me to use in feeding the infant, but unknown to me, it needed to be diluted. The baby spit it up, and the doctor was furious! He demanded I leave the unit. Mortified, humiliated, and so upset with myself, I tried to run away. I called Henry, and through tears, I told him to pick me up from the hospital right away. The hospital was quite far away, in another county, and he knew I was supposed to be there all day. He told me, "Absolutely not! You get back in there and talk this over with your instructor." I had no way of escape, so I went back in and met with her, despite my tearful condition. She was so calm, as she told me not to give up. She said I was an excellent nurse, and anyone would be happy to hire me. Then she told me that the child was fine, with no problems as a result of my mistake, and that the doctor was rightfully being protective of his patient. I couldn't wait to leave! I was sick to my stomach over what had happened! How could I make a mistake like that? I was remorseful and inconsolable. Over the next days and weeks, I made myself physically sick with anxiety. Finally, after several trips to the emergency room, I had missed too many clinical days, and I had to drop out of nursing school. I was only one semester away from graduation. I had destroyed my health with my own guilt and unforgiveness for what I had done. I called Martha, to tell her what had happened. Expecting sympathy, Martha calmly said, "Hannah, that is pride. Are you Jesus Christ?" "No," I responded. "Then why would you ever think that you would never make a mistake?" Her words pierced my heart, and I knew she was right. She told me to "dust myself off," and get back to what God had called me to do. The enemy had whispered defeat in my ears, using my own unforgiveness for what I had done, to end my career before it started. Then, God sent His messenger to speak the truth to me. I did not need sympathy, I needed to hear that I should be pursuing the calling God gave me. Thankfully I did not have to wait long in order to get back in the nursing program. They found an opening for me, by the very next semester! I had a renewed sense of calm, knowing I was where I should be. And finally, I was in my last semester of Nursing School!

Blessings from God

One night we were relaxing at home, when our daughter, Claire and her husband came by. She was beaming and happy, as she gave us a small gift box. The greatest surprise ever, was inside that little box! It was a positive pregnancy test! Claire and her husband had been trying for a long time to have a child, then a miscarriage shattered both of their hearts, and ours too. And now, after so long, a baby was on the way!

I always relished the exciting times we spent together preparing for her wedding, and this was even more exciting! I loved all the plans and shopping for special things for our grandchild, and tried to be involved as much as I could, despite nursing school. Claire was so beautiful with child! She looked so regal and strong; and so very determined to be the best mother she could be. She was devoted to good health, and planned to nurse her baby. I couldn't be, any prouder!

I was honored that she wanted me there when it was her time. I was so proud of her! Her delivery was extremely difficult, with baby in the wrong position. But she persevered, like the warrior she is, and finally, after many hours, her daughter was born! Our first grandchild! She was longed for, prayed for and now after several years, she had finally arrived. I was a grandma! Words cannot describe the feeling of seeing your baby girl, holding her own baby girl. It was one of the most wonderful moments in my life. I was so thankful to be there, and to be a part of that blessed miracle. Being a grandma, was more important to me, than becoming a nurse! And my graduation was only a couple of weeks away.

I felt so blessed that my daughter brought my newborn granddaughter to my graduation! I was also thrilled to have my son and my momma there, along with my good friends, and Martha, my wonderful mentor and counselor. It was a day and night I will always remember! Walking across the field to receive my Bachelor of Science degree in the afternoon, carrying a lighted lamp in the evening, as we recited the Nightingale Pledge, and finally being pinned by my instructor as a Registered Nurse.

I will never forget my daughter's words to me, "Mom, you have always been a nurse, now you just have the paper to prove it."

I was hired right after graduation by the hospital I had hoped for, and in a unit that would be a wonderful base for my eventual career as a Hospice Nurse. A job I treasured as a ministry from God. And that, is another story!

Tragedy Strikes

Several years later, we were led to move from our home, and we all transplanted to a beautiful town with four seasons, another lifelong dream. I was working for a hospice service in town, and our lives were busy with our children and grandchild. Our son had married a girl we adored, and we were involved with their church, one based on the word of God. It was busy, but we were doing fine.

Then I was awakened by a phone call, early in the morning one September. It was my sister, and she was crying. "What's the matter?" I asked, but she had trouble saying it. Finally, she said, "It's our brother, he's gone!"

I tried to stay calm, and I told her I would come as soon as possible. When I hung up, I burst into tears. My precious baby brother was gone!

The sun rose and set on him for me after he was born, when I was almost eight years old. He was the cutest, most active little boy! He fell and hit his forehead as a toddler, and a big goose egg rose up, frightening Momma and me. When we got to the hospital, the nurse thought I was the patient because I was so upset and crying over my baby brother's head injury! It wouldn't be the last goose egg. He was constantly getting hurt, and I worried so much over him. He nearly died at three years old, when a fever sent his temperature to 107 degrees Fahrenheit, and they could not bring his temperature down. They sent him home, instructing my momma how to perform ways to try and keep his fever down. He was not responsive at times, and I never felt so helpless! It took a few days before his fever finally broke.

Despite his sweet, friendly nature, he was teased and picked on as a boy. I never forgot the time that he came crying to Momma, saying, "I just want to be friends! Why won't they play with me?" I wanted to go out and smack every one of those kids! But Momma wouldn't let me. He had a rough time growing up, never finding the friends he so wanted. His teen years led to friendships with the wrong people. He was so eager for friends, he just didn't use good judgement, and fell in with a bad crowd. Momma and Daddy suffered terribly during that time, as they tried to rescue him from trouble. Eventually he did get clean, but was never really able to support himself. Learning disabilities and ADHD, kept him from being successful in the jobs he managed to get. So he was mostly dependent on our folks. The intense devotion I felt for him, faded as Momma would tell me how heartbroken she was over his choices. I felt defensive of my momma, and was angry with him. I tried to be nice, but he could sense my coldness. He really needed my support, and I failed him. He really admired a photo collage I had made for Momma and Daddy's Anniversary the year before, and his birthday was coming, so I made a photo collage for him. I had pictures of him as a boy, photos I had taken with my camera, that he didn't have. And several other good photos. I told him how much I loved him in his birthday card. I never stopped loving him! I was just disappointed in him, when I should have forgiven him, and just loved him. He called me on his birthday to thank me for the gift. He was so happy with it, and he got choked up when I told him I loved him. It would be the last time I would hear his voice. I wish I had kept him on the phone longer. Twelve days later, he was gone.

My parents, brother and sister all lived south of us. So, Henry got me a flight down there the next day. My sister told me that he had been target shooting with a friend on a nearby mountain, with a narrow, two-lane road. They were heading back down when my brother lost control of his pick-up. It slid off the road and went over a cliff. My mind had been racing, wondering how long was he down there? Did he die quickly? How long did it take for emergency responders to get there? I was in a daze as I climbed into my seat in the plane. A nice lady was sitting next to me, and she asked me where I was going. I teared up as I told her. Then she introduced herself, she was a Hospice nurse! The Lord in His mercy chose that seat for me! It felt good to be sitting next to someone who understood my pain.

When I arrived at the airport, I picked up the rental that Henry had reserved for me, and headed swiftly to my parent's home a couple of hours away. I was so anxious to get there! When I arrived, Momma was alone, and I asked her where Daddy was. Through tears she said that he had gone up to the mountain to see where my brother had died. She was worried about him, and so was I! It seemed like forever, before he arrived home. He seemed amazed and bewildered, and his voice was trembling, tears running down his face. "What happened?" We both asked. He said he was standing at the edge of the cliff where his son had died, crying. Then a man came up to him, seemingly out of nowhere, and asked if he was the father of the man who died, and Daddy shook his head yes. Several other people appeared too. Unknown to Daddy, there was a church at the top of the mountain. The man told Daddy he was an off-duty police officer, and they had heard the crash, and ran down to help. Finding my brother's body without a pulse, him and another man began CPR, as the others called for help. They kept up the CPR until the paramedics arrived and he was declared dead. The off-duty police officer hugged Daddy, and prayed for him, along with several others from the church, including an elderly lady. My Daddy, God bless him, is an agnostic by his own admission. And as he stood there telling me and Momma about what happen, he wept, and kept saying, "They prayed for me!" My Daddy was so very touched by that simple gesture!

The story he told, answered so many questions I had! All the way there, I was picturing my brother laying on the side of a cliff, all alone, wondering, "How long did it take for him to die?" God had placed a professional right there to be with him, and he told my Daddy that he was gone when he got to him. I found out later the extent of his injuries, when my poor Momma begged to see her son, or at least hold his hand, and they would not allow it. As a Hospice Nurse, they respected my request to see the coroner's report, and I knew his death had been instantaneous. Momma never got her wish to hold his hand. They had argued just before he left the house, and usually they would resolve it by him kissing her forehead, and her holding his hand. That did not happen this time, he just went out the door, and was gone. I went into Hospice Nurse mode, the moment I arrived, and never allowed my own grief to flow. I was so worried about my momma! She was very ill already, having been quite sick, and losing a lot of weight. She worried over how they could afford a funeral. My sister had arrived, and she was an amazing help for my parents. She handled all of the insurance calls and helped with all the things that were hard for my folks to deal with. Then Momma got a call from the Moose Lodge, where my brother worked, and they told her that they would be providing a memorial service for him at no cost to my parents! They loved him there. He was always such a cheerful guy! He held his sorrow inside, so longing for a wife and children, and a normal life. Life was always just too hard for him. But I took solace in knowing that he loved Jesus! At one point, he was making wooden crosses for people. He loved working with wood. People where he lived then, called him the "Cross Man". He loved that! I have two of the crosses he made. I think that God reached down and scooped up my brother, to save him from the heartache that was his life, and that he is working with his Master Carpenter now. Life here was just too hard for his tender spirit. The memorial service was lovely. They even provided a buffet and there were many beautiful flowers. I was grateful that my daddy's friend, Pat had arrived. He was an elderly man with a chipper personality, and he was a Christian. My daddy really looked up to him, as he was a retired officer, and they had become great friends. I was only able to stay for a week, and knowing that Pat would be in town for a while, helped me be able to say good-bye.

Then I went back home, and to work, and my job suddenly became very difficult for me. For the first time, I was having trouble keeping my job at work, and not bringing it home. My heart was just too tender now, and it showed. I never got the chance to tell my brother that I forgave him, and loved him no matter what he did. Forgiveness is a gift we all need, and one we should all give to our loved ones. I tried to bury my heartache, focusing on work and my family, so grieving my brother would have to wait.

It would be three years before my grief built-up to a point that it could not be ignored. Through the comfort of a grief support group at church, I found the peace I longed for. I still grieve his loss, but knowing he is with Christ, has made all the difference in the world.

Dark Memories Revealed

While I was grieving my brother, there was a much, bigger issue, brewing deep inside, like a volcano as it builds up pressure, before it explodes. Only this would not explode, but rather seep, like molten lava, unannounced, unwanted, like a home invasion. It terrorized me! I had no idea why this was happening, or how to respond.

It started early in the year, with my first panic attack. I was a nurse, and still, I had no idea what was happening! I had never experienced anything like it. My heart suddenly started rapidly pounding, it became hard to breathe, and I felt as if I were going to die, even though I logically knew I would not. I called my daughter, and she recognized the signs of a panic attack, and calmly reassured me that I would be okay, then she prayed for me. She also advised me to call my "daughter-in-love" (What I call her), because she was all too familiar with those episodes, and could be helpful. When I called her, she also calmly reaffirmed what my daughter had said, and she also prayed for me. Then she told me about an acupressure point that can sometimes be helpful. I followed her instructions, and it worked for me. I was relieved, because this happened while I was enjoying a peaceful drive towards home, after a patient visit, and had to pull the car over and stop. I couldn't understand why this happened! I was feeling fine, with no anxious thoughts. It did not make logical sense to me. I checked my vital signs when I got home, and I was fine. It was the first warning of things to come.

A couple of months passed, and I had to attend a Hospice seminar, that triggered deep emotions and melancholy. It led to remembering that sad period when I was a little girl, and was abused. The next day, I prayed for God to make me His vessel, to serve Him. Suddenly, memories that had been buried, oozed out, revealing vile things my birth father had done to me. He had sexually abused me! I felt nauseated, and nearly vomited, my head spinning in disbelief and shock. But I knew that what had been released, was just the beginning, and that more would be uncovered.

The Lord is so merciful! He waited until I was able to bear the memories before He allowed the cleansing of them to begin. He was beginning to cleanse His vessel, to be used by Him. It would take a few years before the Lord shined His light in every dark corner, evicting the stench of rotting, suppressed memories. It would be a long journey.

My first response to these revelations, was anger. I felt so betrayed, and was so angry that someone who was supposed to be my advocate and protector would do such things! But even in my anger, I realized how merciful God was, in waiting until he had passed away, before these things were revealed. I was able to be the very picture of forgiveness and love for him before he died. I knew that I would *not* have been able to do that, if I knew then, what I was finding out now. I remembered that there was abuse, but not the things that were finally being revealed. I found a very helpful Christian book on healing from childhood sexual abuse: *On the Threshold of Hope* by Diane Mandt Langberg, Ph. D. The author wisely instructed readers to only read a short section at a time, to allow time to process. If you are reading this as a survivor of childhood sexual abuse, and you are a Christian, I highly recommend her book. It was so helpful to know that I was not alone, and I was thankful that I only endured six months of abuse, unlike so many who lived all their childhood with abuse. Reading the book, brought more memories, but there was a battle in my mind, between wanting to know, and fearfulness about what would be revealed. Prior to every memory revealed, I would have anxiety symptoms, and dreaded what I would remember next. I had many related dreams as my memories returned, laden with symbolism, so I did not always understand them. Finally, I started seeing a therapist, and she really helped reveal the truth in the dreams. Her understanding and kindness, was invaluable to my healing. I will never forget the question she asked me: "Do you believe Jesus was with you when those things happened?" I was shocked at her question! First, that she was acknowledging my faith in Jesus Christ, but more importantly, it made me really think about it. I could not imagine that He was there, but in my heart of hearts, I knew He was. I knew that He was God, and that God is omnipresent; so, He must have been there! Slowly, I came to realize, that it was my Savior, Jesus, who covered my eyes with His hand, hiding what was happening to me. And now, it was time to bring the memories out into the light.

> *He reveals deep and secret things; He knows what is in the darkness, And light dwells with Him. (Daniel 2:22)*

For there is nothing hidden which will not be revealed, nor has anything been kept secret but that it should come to light.
(Jesus, as quoted in Mark 4:22)

It was during this time that I sought prayer from ladies at church who helped other ladies pray through deep hurts like mine. It was a blessed revelation! As we prayed, they asked me if Jesus was there, and if I could see Him in my spirit. And I did! He was standing so close to me, that His robes would have been touching me, but as I had my head bowed in prayer, I only saw the hem of His robes, and His sandaled feet. His robes were rough and appeared to be "working robes." I understood! Jesus was indeed with me. And He would be right next to me as I went forward in the work of recovery, working along side me, because there was more work to be done. "… I will never leave you or forsake you." (Hebrews 13:5)

This gave me courage as I faced each day. It was a very difficult time for me, as the memories came back in abundance, and I experienced what had happened to me all over again.

It is a horrible feeling to realize that someone who should be loving and protecting you from evil, was sexually abusing you, their own child! I was only four years old during that time, so I had no way to defend myself. I just wanted my momma, but I was being told she wasn't my mother anymore, and I was far from Grandma's farm and my momma. My life had become a nightmare, without the loving family I knew. I shut down mentally, like a walking zombie. I stared blankly, and did not respond to the abuse. I eventually stopped crying. There was no hope, no escape, no love. The only place I felt love was at church. I loved being able to go!

"Jesus loves me, this I know, for the Bible tells me so; Little ones to Him belong, they are weak but He is strong! Yes, Jesus loves me, Yes, Jesus loves me; Yes, Jesus loves me, the Bible tells me so!"

No wonder I loved that song! No wonder I loved going to church! I could feel the love of Christ in the people there! I remember not wanting to leave. I still have the Certificate of Attendance I received from them. My momma saved it, and gave it to me when I was an adult. At that time, I never thought I would see my momma again.

My Sweet Momma

Then, one day, over six months after we were separated, we were finally reunited. Momma was quickly given custody of me, with the evidence of my abuse quite evident. It was not easy for her. I was not functioning normally. I had lost a large portion of my long red hair. She got my hair cut until it could grow back. I remember the beautiful, long drives to the Child Psychologist, located in a beautiful hillside area. Momma said it took almost a year before I was functioning again. She had experienced a nightmare too. She told me many years later about what it was like in prison. Some of the inmates killed a girl right next to Momma, as she trembled in fear on her cot, covering her face with her blanket, trying to block out the horror. A living nightmare, separated from her little daughter and all she loved.

Finally, we were together again! Just me and Momma, struggling to learn how to live and breathe again. Both of us, broken vessels, wounded and on guard. I can't imagine how hard it must have been for her! But she was determined. And fabulous. Her singing! Constant and joyous, she would lead me in song, "Little red caboose, Little red caboose, Little red caboose behind the tra-a-ain!" She sang with gusto as she shuffled her feet, making chugging sounds down the sidewalk with me on the way home from school. My "Glamorous Ma", as her daddy, called her, so concerned with her image, dropping all pretense, to bring joy into my life.

At bath time, she made it fun for me, by singing, "This is the way we wash our face, Wash our face, Wash our face, This is the way we wash our face, So early in the morning..." She sang through the whole bath.

She was working in a factory, and didn't make much, but still, she bought me a Little Golden Book every payday. I loved those books, and buried myself in the stories every chance I got. She also took me to the massive, beautiful, downtown library, where I couldn't wait to look for another darling Beatrix Potter book to read! She taught me sweetly, naturally, every waking moment, about plants, flowers, bugs, trees, proper grammar, and how to be a lady. She always displayed perfect English, manners and graciousness, showing me by example, an example I still try to live up to. I remember how grown up and beautiful I felt, as she taught me how to walk with a book on my head, and I did it! I was so proud, and felt so treasured.

She was a wonderful, devoted mother to me, and to my brother and sister when they came along. Our health, protection and well-being were her primary goals. She excelled at cooking nutritious, delicious meals, was an impeccable homemaker, who kept her home beautiful and "as clean as a whistle!" She performed all her tasks joyfully, singing her way through every chore. But her greatest love besides her family, was gardening. It was where she went to unwind and relished putting her hands in the dirt. She could grow anything! When I would go out to talk to her, she always explained about what she was doing, the name of the plants she was working with, and what was needed to keep them healthy. I didn't really care, then. But everything she taught me, stayed secure in my memory. The names of plants and flowers came easily to me as an adult, because she had imprinted them on my heart.

It was in September, last year, that I quickly planted 72 bulbs, trying to beat the first frost. I managed to cover them all with a light layer of autumn leaves to protect them from the cold. I wanted to make Momma proud of me. I have never had the urge to garden. But since we downsized to our little cottage, gardening seems more attainable, with less garden to manage. A freeze came the next day, after putting those bulbs to bed for winter, when I got the news.

My sweet momma had fallen and broken her hip. She passed away a few weeks later, but not until after I had journeyed to her bedside to see her, and helped my daddy and sister with placement in an Adult Family Home, on Hospice care. I praise God that I was able to see her! And that she recognized me, her eyes bright with recognition, smiling joyfully as she saw me! I am so thankful! I was there a week before heading back home; knowing she would not be with us much longer, but that she was in good hands. A few weeks later she passed away peacefully just after midnight, carried home to Jesus, just as she longed to be! She had told me a few years ago, that she just wanted to go home to Jesus. It is so hard for those with dementia, knowing that there is something wrong, and unable to understand what is happening to them. My very strong, determined momma, was so fragile and weak before she slipped away. Still, she was beautiful, with a shining smile, and white crown of fluffy hair. I have comforted others, so many times as a Hospice Nurse, but this, this was my own, precious momma! My sweet savior, defender, encourager, teacher, mentor, comforter, healer, and my bright, shining example of a Proverbs 31 woman.

I pray that I can be half the woman my mother was! She leaves a legacy that is hard to match.

I am praising God for His merciful kindness to me during the last year, especially during the holidays. I thought Thanksgiving and Christmas would be really difficult for me; instead, the Lord flooded my heart with the loving kindness of the body of Christ, my loving family and so many wonderful memories of my momma and all that she did for me. I still have moments of sorrow and profound loss, but the Lord is always there to comfort me and count my tears. What a good, good Father!

You number my wanderings;
Put my tears into Your bottle;
Are they not in Your book?
(Psalm 56:8)

Forgive as We Have Been Forgiven

I am no longer angry about my birth father. It took a few years for me to process all of the dark memories that came to light. My anger was slowly washed away, as the mercy and comfort of Christ led me to His forgiveness. I could never come to that place without His loving guidance. Being reconciled to my birth father, his sweet wife, and my siblings, was a pivotal point in my life, despite the truth that came to light afterwards. When we were reunited, they joyfully, lovingly, welcomed me in with open arms, and I forgave all; because Christ had forgiven me!

I believe in my heart, that my father accepted forgiveness in Christ before he died. The Lord has given me peace about him, and I trust in the Lord's mercy.

Our time here on earth is so short and full of trials; we all suffer so much! But the Lord Jesus took all of our sins upon Himself, to redeem us back to Him! So, we should forgive the hurts and the people who hurt us, just as Christ forgave us. This is how those who don't know Him, will be able to see Him, through us! Some hurts are far worse than what I experienced; some are less. Only the Lord Jesus can give us the grace, the mercy, and the heart to forgive them. I could not, we cannot, without the power of the Holy Spirit who leads us, through the Lord Jesus Christ. He calls us to forgive. Just as He forgave us.

For if you forgive men their trespasses, your heavenly Father will also forgive you. (Jesus, as quoted in Matthew 6:14)

I pray that this account will serve to help others in their struggles to overcome unforgiveness, and to know that they are not alone! The Lord is with you, and He will carry you too, through your journey to forgiveness.

For I will forgive their iniquity, and their sin I will remember no more. (Jeremiah 31:34b)

About the Author

A sinner, saved by grace in 1971, Hannah has journaled her blessings, heartaches and prayers to her Savior ever since. As a wife, mother, grandmother and retired Registered Nurse, her call has always been to encourage others with the mercy and love of Christ. She enjoys writing uplifting devotions online and serves on the Care Team at her church.